Cherry on Top

BOBBIE
Cherry on Top
Flirty, Forty-Something, and Funny as F**k
BROWN

with **Caroline Ryder**

A BARNACLE BOOK | RARE BIRD BOOKS
LOS ANGELES, CALIF.

THIS IS A GENUINE BARNACLE BOOK

A Barnacle Book | Rare Bird Books
453 South Spring Street, Suite 302
Los Angeles, CA 90013
rarebirdbooks.com

For more information, address:
A Barnacle Book | Rare Bird Books Subsidiary Rights Department
453 South Spring Street, Suite 302
Los Angeles, CA 90013

Set in Dante
Printed in the United States

Photographs Courtesy of Bobbie Brown

10 9 8 7 6 5 4 3 2 1

Publisher's Cataloging-in-Publication Data
Names: Brown, Bobbie, 1969–, author. | Ryder, Caroline, author.
Title: Cherry on Top: Flirty, Forty-Something, and Funny as F**k / by Bobbie Jean Brown, with Caroline Ryder.
Description: First Hardcover Edition | A Barnacle Book | New York, NY; Los Angeles, CA: Rare Bird Books, 2019.
Identifiers: ISBN 9781644280157
Subjects: LCSH Brown, Bobbie, 1969– | Actors—United States—Biography. | Rock musicians' spouses—United States—Biography. | Models (Persons)—United States—Biography. | BISAC BIOGRAPHY & AUTOBIOGRAPHY / Rich & Famous. | BIOGRAPHY & AUTOBIOGRAPHY / Entertainment & Performing Arts.
Classification: LCC PN2287.B6965 C44 2019 | DDC 791.4302/8092—dc23

Dedicated to my supportive loving family, friends, and fans.
Thank you for loving me even when I don't love myself.
I'm blessed to have you all. XO.

LIFE'S A GAS

I T WAS AROUND MIDNIGHT on a Tuesday and moonlight crept over Arleta, the quiet LA suburb I call home. These days, I sleep alone in my four-poster bed—unless you count Nupa, my ten-year-old Chihuahua. After years of sharing me with various male interlopers, Nupa was pleased to finally have me to herself. She lay on the bed, watching me as I gathered clothes from around my bedroom, a little snaggletooth protruding from her lower jaw. During quiet days at home like this one, I'd catch myself thinking about Josh, the musician sixteen years younger than myself with whom I'd spent the last five years of my life.

An ex-Mormon who worked in construction, Josh had a band whose goals, according to their social media pages, included "waking up in the van covered in glitter in front of a church on Easter morning after a long night of swimming in Jack Daniel's and getting some strange." Marriage material, if you're me. My daughter, Taylar, who is an excellent judge of character, loathed Josh so much she sent him a bag of dirt for Christmas one year. Yes, Josh had more red flags than a Communist parade, but I was blinded by his long brown hair, lazy smile, and slender body, which took me back to a different time in my life. A time when the Sunset Strip still had a pulse. A time when life was a beautiful mess of music, love, and hairspray.

I stuffed my dirty laundry in the basket and stomped down the beige-carpeted stairs, scolding myself for missing Josh and swearing I would never again date *anyone* who is a fan of Mötley Crüe. In a Mötley fan's mind, you see, sleeping with me takes them one step closer to being Tommy Lee, to whom I was engaged many moons ago. *Well, guess what, you'll never be Tommy Lee*, I fumed. *And if you were, I sure as hell wouldn't date you.*

Distracted by my thoughts, I misjudged a step. My slipper flew off my foot and I tumbled down the stairs, headfirst into the corner of a marble side table. Laundry went flying and there was a thud as I hit the floor, and for one terrifying moment, the whole world turned black. Slowly, I opened my eyes. Psychedelic globes bounced lazily about my field of vision like an old screensaver. Whimpering, I felt for my cell phone in the back pocket of my jeans and dialed my younger brother, Adam, who lived a few blocks away with his wife, Laura, and their baby, Ollie.

"Adam, help," I whispered, as Nupa hopped down the stairs and gave me a look of concern.

When Adam arrived at my condo, he gasped; I looked like Rocky Balboa after twelve rounds with a meat grinder.

He helped me into his car and drove me to the emergency room, urging me to stay awake, promising me that everything was going to be okay. Adam was my lifeline, my only family in Los Angeles, though I worried that he and his wife were growing weary of Lonely Aunt Bobbie visiting every day, clinging to their newborn infant with tears in her eyes for reasons no one quite understood.

At the hospital, the neurologist told me that fifty percent of people who hit their heads as hard as I did wind up in the morgue. Had the marble side table impacted my head just three millimeters to the left, it would have ruptured some vital vein whose name escapes me, resulting in instant death. I was lucky to be alive, even though my skull ached with indescribable pain and a bump the size of a softball began taking shape on my forehead.

"Off topic," said the doctor, "but…are you the 'Cherry Pie' girl?"

I nodded, trying not to rattle my tenderized brain.

"I thought so!" he exclaimed. "Wow, you really were an It Girl back then. I had the biggest crush on you!"

I was an It Girl, once. Miss Bobbie Jean Brown, Southern pageant queen, runner-up in Miss Teen USA 1987, and for a minute, the hottest girl on the Sunset Strip. "Helter skelter in a summer swelter," I was built for stonewashed jeans and stadium rock, with my long legs, sun-kissed hair, and a smile that lit up rooms. Secretly, I always wished I looked like one of those waifish brunettes, the kind you see on the Paris runway, but the reflection in the mirror confirmed that, in the words of Raymond Chandler, "it was a blonde." And in LA, people want blondes. Casting agents want them. Bands want them. Men want them.

For fifteen years, during the peak of my good fortune, I had my pick of rich and famous lovers. When I met Rod Stewart at the Roxbury, he asked me what I wanted—I told him a cranberry vodka, and he laughed, "No, I meant Ferrari, Porsche, or Jaguar?" Strangers would approach me in clubs, offer me $100,000 to spend the night with them—and if only I hadn't been so principled, I might have moved up the property ladder by now.

Romance came thick and fast. I spent several coked-up months with Rob from Milli Vanilli, enjoyed dance-floor flirtations with Prince, shared intimate moments with a Chippendale in a broom closet, brushed off overtures from O. J. Simpson, spent dreamy nights on ecstasy with Dave Navarro, shared kisses at the Chateau Marmont with Ethan Hawke, and experienced a titanic roll in the hay with Leonardo DiCaprio. We mustn't forget the night I set Kevin Costner's bedroom on fire. Literally. Nor the strange, chaotic year I spent engaged to my teen idol, Tommy Lee, drummer of the most notorious rock band on the Strip: Mötley Crüe.

But it was my marriage to blond, blue-eyed singer Jani Lane of the hair band Warrant that caused middle-aged neurologists to recognize me in hospitals. You see, in 1990, Jani handpicked me to star in the video for one of the biggest songs of the decade, "Cherry Pie," which placed my all-American body on heavy rotation on MTV, VH1, and television screens all over the world.

Overnight, Jani and I became sweetheart darlings of rock 'n' roll, on- and off-screen. We were the perfect match—I was the fun-loving, bubblegum-chewing girl of his melancholic dreams, the bombshell who could shock him into laughter. That's the thing: beautiful blondes are everywhere in Hollywood, but try finding one who can make you laugh.

On *The Howard Stern Show*, Jani announced to the world that he was going to marry me. His public devotion and chivalry won me over, and after making love on the bullet train in Tokyo, I became pregnant with our baby girl, Taylar Jayne Lane. Four months later, on July 15, 1991, we married on the rooftop of the Wyndham Bel Age Hotel, the air heavy with the scent of five hundred pink roses and several dozen cans of Elnett. All our friends came to the wedding—Guns n' Roses's Duff McKagan, Def Leppard's Rick Allen, and my dance-floor buddy, R&B singer Bobby Brown. Our wedding was a fitting climax to the perfect Sunset Strip fairytale—even though behind the scenes, the cracks in my relationship with Jani were already starting to show, and the Sunset Strip was inching closer and closer to implosion. It didn't matter what the future held, though, because from that day on, my fate was sealed.

I would forever be the Cherry Pie Girl.

✳✳✳

WHEN I CAME HOME from the hospital after my tumble down the stairs, I cried like a baby, and not just because I looked like the Elephant Man. It was a slap in the face, a reminder of how unraveled my life had become. I was that old Hollywood cliché—the small-town blonde, fallen from grace, her fifteen minutes long behind her. Hollywood had made me pay the price for the hubris of my youth. Over and over again I'd been knocked down, passed over, and dismissed as too old, too fat, too loud, too Bobbie. Blonde hair and a quick wit no longer opened doors for me. In the past five years alone my TV show had been canceled, my agent had dropped me, my body ached because of a traumatic car accident, and I'd endured the most humiliating breakup of my life with Josh, who, it turned out, was secretly sending high-resolution photographs of his dick to every girl in LA with a cell phone and data plan. On top of all this, wildfires were circling the city, temperatures were rising, the ice caps were melting, and so were my breast implants. Then I heard someone say rock 'n' roll was over—"bye, bye, Miss American Pie," might as well throw yourself down the stairs.

For weeks, the bruise bulged out of my head, protruding like a unicorn's horn, a reminder of how alone I was in the world. What if my brother hadn't been there to take me to the hospital? Who could I count on? Most of my immediate family lived far away in Baton Rouge, Louisiana. I had no husband, no boyfriend. Yes, I had friends, but friends got busy. My home seemed unsafe, a place where bad things might happen. I trod carefully down the stairs, stopped doing laundry at midnight, and installed a Nest Cam. Mentally, I felt like a senior citizen with brittle bones and one foot in the grave even though I hadn't even turned fifty.

Then came yet another blow, one that hit even harder than my fall: my brother told me he was moving. Not to another neighborhood, to another planet. Planet Minnesota. I understood the sane, pragmatic reasons why my sane, pragmatic brother was leaving Hollywood; it was expensive now, prohibitively so, and there was no way he could afford to buy or even rent a home fit for raising his family here. Adam, like so many others, was about to become an unwilling economic exile of Los Angeles, whose blushing sunsets have been marred by the shadows of wage stagnation, rent hikes, and social inequality. The American Dream was out of reach for Adam in this town, but it could still happen for him in the Midwest.

The day before they left, I promised to entertain my nephew while Adam and his wife supervised the movers who were loading their stuff into trucks. Watching them, I grew emotional. I couldn't stand the thought that this might be the last time in months I'd get to hold my little nephew. I couldn't stop the tears, so I asked my brother if I could go home for an hour to calm myself down.

"Of course, Bobbie," he said.

I fell asleep crying in my bed and woke up two hours later to messages from Adam's wife, Laura. They'd had to leave already and were checking in to a hotel by the airport. I begged for one last dinner together with them like we did every Sunday. But it was too late; Ollie was asleep. They promised to text me in the morning and arrange to meet so we could say goodbye in person. But in the end there was no time, and I didn't get to hug my brother, or Laura, or worst of all, my nephew. I so wanted to tell him that his auntie loved him very much, that he brought joy to my world, that I felt alive playing with him, enjoying his perfect little soul. I didn't get to say any of that.

After they left, I looked at myself in the mirror, at the dent in my forehead, a permanent reminder of the night I fell. That incident had felt like a fork in the road, yet months later, here I was, still lingering at the crossroads, unsure of which way to go. My brother's departure felt like another prod from above. *Why are you still in Los Angeles, Bobbie Brown? What are you doing here? What's your purpose?* Should I go back to Baton Rouge? Follow my brother to Minnesota? Should I just remain a widowed bride of Los Angeles until the day I die?

This city had once felt so full of promise to me. At twenty-one, I walked the Strip like it was my own personal catwalk. At forty-eight, with a dent in my head and enough baggage to fill a cross-country freight train, it seemed like maybe it was finally time to pack up my hair extensions and call it a day.

Looking at my reflection in the mirror, I hated what I saw: a fallen starlet whose life looked like one huge, long joke. I was a promising career littered with fumbled opportunities, a love life where each lapse of judgement was grander and more ridiculous than the last. It was bad punchline after bad punchline, and I'd had enough. *You're not a joke, Bobbie, you're not a joke,* I told my reflection firmly.

Then it hit me. I'd been seeing it all wrong. I *am* a joke. A really, really funny one. I've just never gotten 'round to telling it!

FUNNILY ENOUGH...

IN 1995, TOMMY LEE got high on ecstasy and married Pamela Anderson on a beach in Cancún four days after he and I called off our engagement. That's when I first considered pursuing comedy professionally.

I'd always been known as a funny girl—in high school, the teachers would put my desk in the hallway to keep me from distracting the class with my wisecracks. My mom, Judy, always said to me, "You can turn a dumpy day into sunshine, Bobbie." And Sharise Neil, ex-wife of Mötley Crüe singer Vince Neil and my ride-or-die bestie for nearly thirty years, had been telling me for ages I should give comedy a go.

"Yes, you're beautiful," she once told me, "but you also talk about diarrhea in a really funny way."

Sharise thought I should star in rom-coms or have a sitcom like *Seinfeld*. In the early 2000s, thanks to the encouragement of my loved ones, I finally drummed up the courage to audition for the Groundlings, one of the best improv schools in the world. And to my surprise, they loved me. I nailed the audition. I couldn't believe it.

At the time, I was dating Jay Gordon, singer of the industrial band Orgy. Jay had spiky silver hair, wore cyber-goth platform boots, and shaved his eyebrows. Taylar, who was around eight years old at the time, refused to be seen with Jay in public. She called him Frankenscissors because to her he looked like a cross between Frankenstein and Edward Scissorhands. She thought Jay was a dork, but as usual, I was utterly impervious to her good advice.

"Jay, I auditioned for the Groundlings, and I got in!" I told him when I got home, so proud to have been accepted.

Jay looked at me, bored. He always looked bored. "But you're not funny, Bobbie."

"I'm not?"

"Nope."

He's right, whispered the voice in my head. *You're just some dumb blonde who can't keep a man. What's funny about that?*

I never went back to the Groundlings. Self-sabotage is a career choice too.

In 2015, I tried once again, gingerly, to explore the idea of being funny for money. I went to the Comedy Store, where a few friends were doing stand-up. After the show, I asked their advice on breaking in and the responses were overwhelmingly negative.

"Don't do it, Bobbie."

"This is a really hard field to get into."

Et cetera.

I didn't have to read too far between the lines to understand what they were saying: I was too old to hack it. It was too late in the game. I was already in my mid-forties, and my chances of failure were 100 percent. But there's nothing like a near-fatal fall down the stairs to kickstart your career goals. I no longer cared that Jay "Frankenscissors" Gordon didn't think I was funny. I didn't care that comedy was a tough field to get into or that I was older than most people starting out on that stage. This time, I was giving comedy a shot.

I called Jerod Zavistoski—an actor, male dating coach, and comedian—who had interviewed me on his podcast, Modern Male Radio, several times. I told him I had been thinking about trying stand-up comedy and asked if he could give me any pointers. He invited me to accompany him to a comedy class in Hollywood and see what I thought. His teacher was a man called Jimmy Shin, a booker at the Comedy Store and the Hollywood Improv. Sort of like the Yoda of the Comedy Strip, he and his teaching partner Gary Robinson are known for helping young—I mean *aspiring*—comedians break into the game.

Jerod showed me into the class. "Everyone, this is Bobbie Brown, the Cherry Pie Girl!"

I rolled my eyes. Something about being introduced as Cherry Pie Girl makes me feel uncomfortable, like I'm supposed to leap into character and do a little dance.

"Pleased to meet you," I said, shaking Jimmy's hand, feeling all the eyes in the room upon me.

"I'm glad you're here, Bobbie," said Jimmy, kind and supportive right away. He told me that the reason he started the class was to find new talent and bring that talent into the clubs he booked. Most of his students came to him through referrals.

"The fact that you're here means you're already funny, Bobbie," he said, reassuringly. "All you need is a little help."

Jerod had told me to bring some set-up ideas, or premises, for jokes. Premise, tagline, punchline—that's the way a joke is broken down. I knew that already, so I'd prepared a few set-up ideas about my dating life, which is at its core quite laughable, and with the class's help I figured out some pretty good punchlines. I liked this comedy world with its peculiar language and passionate community. And did you know that comedy groupies are called "chucklefuckers"? I wondered if one day, in the distant future, I, too, would have some chucklefuckers of my own lining up outside the stage door, hopeful for a kiss. I mean, it's gotta be better than Tinder, right?

As the class progressed, I shed my inhibitions. My stories grew wilder and more crass as I dug deep into my imagination, ad-libbing about disastrous, quasi-revolting dating scenarios that had my classmates laughing but also probably wondering if I needed psychological help. I didn't let myself worry about being judged, though. That's what had held me back all these years. From now on, I was going to be all me, all the time.

Afterward, Jimmy pulled me aside for a chat. "Well, you're a natural," he said.

"I am?"

"Yes. All you have to do is talk, and it's funny. Have you thought about breaking down parts of your life story and putting that into your stand-up? You know, all the guys, the Sunset Strip, the juice?"

I wasn't so sure about that. Telling stories about my past, my heartbreaks, my addictions, my failures—that didn't seem too funny to me. I told Jimmy that for now I'd stick to jokes about awkward dates with strange, imaginary men.

During my third class, Jimmy dropped a bombshell.

"You're ready," he said.

I didn't understand what he meant.

"To perform," he said. "At the Comedy Store."

"What? Hell no!" Was he nuts? Even Jerod seemed surprised. There are secrets, theories, and techniques to comedy, things to practice and perfect—two weeks in, how the fuck could he think I was ready to get on stage under a spotlight in front of a paying audience? I shook my head. Nope. Too soon.

"Bobbie, trust me, you can do this," Jimmy said, getting his phone out and typing a message.

"There. You're on the schedule. Comedy Store. Friday night. Be there."

***

If you've ever cruised along the Strip's two and a half miles, you'll know it has two beating hearts: The Rock 'n' Roll Strip and the Comedy Strip. The rock section comprised the Roxy, the Rainbow Bar and Grill, and the

Whiskey A-Go-Go. It was the stomping ground of The Doors and Led Zeppelin in the sixties, the New York Dolls and The Stooges in the seventies, and glam metal bands like Quiet Riot, Mötley Crüe, Ratt, LA Guns, and Warrant in the eighties. But then something happened. Alongside the cute, long-haired boys in denim and leather, young comedians were building a scene of their own just a few feet down the street at the Laugh Factory and the iconic Comedy Store, which was run by the late great Mitzi Shore, mother of Pauly Shore.

Under her stewardship, the Comedy Store became a training ground for stars like Robin Williams, Eddie Murphy, Jim Carrey, Richard Pryor, Whoopi Goldberg, Sam Kinison, Dave Chapelle, Roseanne Barr, Andy Kaufman…all of them and their chucklefuckers were out there rubbing shoulders with the wild-haired guitar guys and their groupies on the Strip. Rock 'n' roll and Laughter, the two opposite sides of the Sunset Strip coin—although, in the twenty-first century, it seems like comedy has overtaken rock 'n' roll as the big ticket. These days, there are bigger crowds lined up to hear the comedians than the guys with guitars.

***

ON THE DAY OF my first comedy show, a strange pall hung over Hollywood, some portent of rain. I was exhausted— the night before, I'd sat in my bedroom writing jokes until dawn, scrambling for ideas, praying to the omnipotent Comedy Goddess in the clouds. These would be the first jokes I ever told in public, on a stage. And not just any stage—*the* stage—so they had better be good. As dawn broke, I dug into the deepest crevasses of my psyche, searching for the little gold nuggets of comedy glimmering in the psychic mud, the jokes that would reintroduce me to the world and help me believe I still had a reason to be here.

I turned onto Selma Avenue, and gasped at what I saw—tent after tent after tent, a sprawling homeless encampment. Upturned shopping carts. A man urinating, another buying drugs in plain view. This wasn't a favela, a refugee camp, or a slum. This was Hollywood, yards away from the Walk of Fame, and it had turned into the gates of hell for these people. I drove by, feeling guilty about my problems, which suddenly seemed so trivial in the face of this crisis. What had happened? This town used to be different; you could be an artist with no money, and still make something happen, still have some place to live. These days, either you're broke or you're rich. After seeing what was happening here, I worried about the future. God, I wish I would have saved money, been smarter. I might have felt more secure had I fallen for Rod Stewart instead of a broke millennial with a dick-pic habit. Hindsight's twenty-twenty.

I arrived at the Comedy Store and looked at the line-up for the Belly Room. Normally, rookies are put on the bill way early or way late, but they'd scheduled me to perform right before the headliner, at peak comedy time, when the room would be packed and expectations would be highest. *Shit.* Backstage, I saw Jimmy. He could tell I was on the verge of a meltdown.

"Don't worry, Bobbie, nerves are normal. You'd have to check your pulse if you didn't feel some anxiety about facing a bunch of strangers and having to make them laugh."

"Thanks, Jimmy."

He placed a reassuring hand on my shoulder. "Guess what! Show's sold out! Because of *you.*"

"It is?"

"Yeah," he said. "People want you to win, Bobbie. Do you want to win?"

I heard the MC call my name.

"Bestselling author, Cherry Pie Girl, nineties babe, and reality-TV star Bobbie Brown...ON STAGE FOR THE FIRST TIME EVER!"

I walked over to the mic, aware of the frantic pounding inside my ribcage. *First, I'll hit them with the one about the scary blowjob, then the bit about my mom screaming in the parking lot, and I'll close with the thing about the butt parasites.* I looked at the crowd; they were clapping and smiling. Jimmy was right. They did want me to win.

"Hello, everyone," I said. "I'm Bobbie Brown, and I'm no longer following my heart because that bitch gives bad directions."

All seemed to be going well. Then, a few jokes in, something very strange happened to me. It felt like I evaporated, left my body somehow. Physically, I was there, telling stories and making people laugh, because there's video footage confirming it. But in that moment, my consciousness just sort of...left the building, rising up like a helium balloon, far above Los Angeles. Finally, I understood the blank, stunned look you sometimes see on young comedians' faces, the equivalent of a "Be Back Soon" sign on a shop window. It's the look that means "I'm so fucking scared, I vacated my body." I'd only ever experienced that feeling once before. On the 134, as my car spun out of control, I left my body, and only vaguely heard my own voice, screaming, "NO, NOT NOW!"

Suddenly, I zoomed back to earth, aware that I was on stage at the Comedy Store with a lot of people sitting in front of me, laughing. I wondered if anyone had noticed that I'd temporarily left the planet. I wound up the joke, thanked the audience, and ran off the stage, where Jimmy was waiting for me.

"You still had a few minutes of time, Bobbie, why did you come off early?" I looked at him, feeling a little spooked.

"Something weird happened to me out there, Jimmy. I lost all sense of time and space."

Jimmy nodded. "Oh, you blacked out. Happens all the time. It's the adrenaline."

Oh. I exhaled, glad that my temporary delirium was nothing out of the ordinary. I asked him if he could tell I wasn't quite in the room the whole time, and he shrugged.

"Well, you did have a bit of a strange look on your face," he said. "Like, surprised. And your movements were kind of jerky, like you were trying to restrain the mic. But don't worry, Bobbie, you were good. Really good!"

I nodded, taking his word for it, as the beautiful realization dawned—after all these years of talking about it, I'd finally popped my comedy cherry.

OUT OF THE VORTEX, INTO THE HOLE

Looking back on the story of your life, it's funny discerning the high points from the low, connecting the dots, and realizing how the tiniest decisions can lead to such cataclysmic shifts in fortunes. People talk about rock bottoms, and mine came after Tommy and I split in 1995. It lasted a solid ten years, during which time I went from It Girl to Shit Girl as crystal meth pulled me into its horrible white vortex. People ask me how I stopped after such a long period of addiction, and I tell them the truth: it's an ongoing battle. I can't say there aren't times when I fall off the wagon. Usually, it happens when I feel pain. When I can't handle my feelings. Using drugs is rarely celebratory for me, you see—I use them because I hurt. That's why I have to be really careful about getting close to people who are bad for me. When I do, I'm literally toying with my life. Because when people let me down, I self-destruct. The difference now is that if I find myself dipping back in, it doesn't last long. My lifestyle is different from what it was twenty years ago. I'm not modeling, I don't go to clubs or bars, and I don't feel pressure to be stick-thin. I'm not in a place to easily adopt a heavy drug user's lifestyle. Besides, I have bigger fish to fry.

That said, even after I pulled myself out of the darkest phase of my addiction, I was still lost. Still hiding myself in bad love. Still wasting time and avoiding doing the work that my talents required of me. I kept my dreams in a box for many years, too frightened to let them out in case no one believed in them. But dreams don't like being boxed. They'll start making noise if you keep them locked up for too long.

***

IN 2015, I WAS driving on the 134, heading toward Downtown LA and cruising in my cute stick-shift 2006 Pontiac Solstice convertible. I must have been going seventy when all of a sudden, my car jerked violently to the right. Something must have hit me from the left; why else would my car veer like that? I started spinning backward toward the median in big circles really fast. I gripped the steering wheel, helpless. Time warped as the whole world turned into a terrifying slow-motion horror movie. This was it. The end. Minutes, hours could have passed as my car spun. I closed my eyes and screamed, "No, not now!" Then my car slammed into the middle divider between the two sides of the freeway.

I should have been dead. For a second, I thought I was. Only the pain convinced me that I wasn't. I saw a man's face pressed up against my window. He yanked open the driver side door and asked me, "Are you okay?"

"No," I said. All the bones on my right side felt broken, as did my left arm and wrist. But I was alive. Someone, something must have heard me scream. I noticed another man standing by his car on the other side of the freeway. Panic welled inside me.

"Did I hit him? Did he hit me? Is he okay? What happened?"

"He's fine," said the stranger, helping me out of my car. "I saw what happened. Your vehicle just lost control. Nobody hit anyone."

I asked this kind man to call Josh. Things were good between us then. We knew our respective roles in the relationship, and our dysfunctions were largely compatible. Romantic codependence had helped us avoid the individual work we needed to do to progress in our own lives, and as far as toxic fantasies went, it worked pretty well. I was the breadwinner, the caretaker, the initiator, the aggressor. I was me on steroids, fulfilling the role of the man of the house with a pet who adored me— and I don't mean Nupa. It was a devil's bargain, of course. The balance of power in love is a delicate thing, and I had yet to grasp just how devastating it is when one partner cultivates weakness in the other, knowingly or otherwise.

An ambulance arrived, as did the police, who examined the scene and concluded I was lucky to be alive. My health insurance didn't cover transportation to the emergency room, and I couldn't afford a thousand-dollar ambulance ride, so Josh drove me to the hospital in the worst pain I have ever experienced. My wrist, my arm, and all my ribs were broken. I was sent home with a cast on my arm and a pair of crutches. For months, I couldn't cough, get up, adjust myself, or turn my head without whimpering in pain. Worst of all, I couldn't laugh.

For months after the accident, every day was the same: wake up, eat, take more sleep and pain pills, and go right back to sleep. When I was finally able to move around by myself, I kept getting stuck. If I squatted down to pick something up off the floor, chances were that I wasn't getting back up. More than once, Josh came home to find me stuck on the floor of my closet, sobbing. For someone like me, so used to being independent, large and in charge, immobility was the cruelest monster I'd ever met.

As the weeks stretched into months, the strain began to wear on me and Josh. I had always been responsible for the bills, but now I couldn't work. He had just lost his job. The physiotherapy and healthcare bills were mounting, and all the money I had earned in my three years on *Ex Wives of Rock* and from my first book, *Dirty Rocker Boys,* was being swallowed up by the costs of getting me back on my feet. Welcome to American healthcare, a black hole designed to consume every last dime in your savings account.

The police report came back. Because there was no proof that I had been hit, they decided that the accident must have been caused by negligence on my part, which meant my car insurer was under no obligation to cover any of my costs. I called my insurer in tears. We went back and forth until finally they agreed to give me money for the totaled car, but nothing toward my healthcare.

One day I was on my computer and a pop-up ad appeared. "If you have a GM car and have been in an accident, click here." I clicked on the link and learned that General Motors, which owned Pontiac, was being sued for billions and was recalling certain vehicles with a 2003–2007 model year. Some of these vehicles had a condition with the ignition switch that would suddenly turn off the engine. The article said nearly one and a half million GM cars were at risk and that the recall condition "may have caused or contributed to at least thirteen front-seat fatalities." I did more digging and found that there had been *nine* recalls on the make and year of my vehicle, which taken together could cause the ignition to shut off, even at high speeds, if there was anything heavier than a key on the keychain. Imagine throwing your car into park when you're going seventy miles per hour. It's going to jerk wildly, a tiny car at high speed, spinning out of control on the freeway, as time slows down to a crawl...

Finally, my car insurer sent me money to the tune of ten thousand dollars for the totaled car—a fraction of what the accident had cost me to that point, but a welcome cash injection nonetheless. Josh and I decided to use the insurance money to purchase a new car so he could drive for Lyft and Uber to support us while I recuperated. One day, I mentioned that I would be needing the new car later that week, but Josh said no. I pointed out that I didn't need his permission to drive my own fucking car.

"It's not your car, Bobbie, it's *my* car," he said.

I demanded he hand me the spare key immediately, pointing out that it was *my* money that had paid for the car. We fought all day, and still, he refused to give me the keys. The power balance had shifted, and the days of our happy dysfunction were over. Each argument grew viler than the last. I started to hate him, but I needed him, and the cycle grew more poisonous with every passing day.

"PUT THE FUCKING BREADSTICKS IN THE FUCKING REFRIGERATOR, BOBBIE!"

It had come to this. My cute millennial boyfriend had turned on me, screaming at me and calling me names because we'd gone out to dinner and I'd forgotten to put the leftovers in the fridge. I picked up breadsticks and sent them flying in the air toward his head. As they made contact, I could see the truth in his eyes. This wasn't what he'd signed up for. His hot, older blonde with a rock 'n' roll pedigree was now a needy invalid on crutches whom he was responsible for. The spell was broken. After the breadsticks happened, we started sleeping apart. Never again would I share a bed with Josh.

***

MY BODY ACHED. I FELT like an old, out-of-tune piano. So, when the TV show *Botched* called to say they wanted me, believe me, it felt like a blessing of the highest order. I know, I know, being invited to appear on a show about plastic surgery fuck-ups might not sound like everybody's idea of good news, but for me at that time, it was a lifeline. It was a return to work, plus a chance to get my body retuned, for free. I was so excited for a fresh start. I wanted the cameras on me again. I wanted to feel beautiful, not like the useless wreck Josh rolled his eyes at every day.

The show's producers told me I needed to undergo a set of tests with their medical team to confirm I was in good health, then we'd be good to go and they'd start fixing my breast implants. I took the tests, excited for my small-screen comeback. A few days later, the show doctor called with some unexpected news.

"Bobbie, I'm afraid you have syphilis."

"*Syphilis*? Are you nuts? There must be some mistake!"

"No, your test came back positive. It's still in the first phase, so you should seek treatment immediately. Unfortunately, your STD diagnosis means you're no longer eligible to appear on the show."

"I can't believe this," I said. "And I'm so confused. I've only been with one person in the last five years. This isn't possible!"

"Well, you might want to have a conversation with that person, Bobbie," the doctor said. "We're very sorry."

I went home and told Josh.

"They must have made a mistake," he said, coolly.

"It's a *medical show*, fucker. How could they make a mistake? Who have you been sleeping with, Josh?"

He paced the room, his eyes flashing. "I've done a lot of messed up things, Bobbie, but I've never had sex with anyone else. Which begs the question—how did *you* get it, huh?"

"I never cheated on you!" I screamed. "You know I haven't!"

My STD diagnosis prompted the biggest, ugliest fight we'd ever had. The mistrust that had been simmering since I discovered he had sent women naked pictures had erupted into full-blown hatred. One of us was lying, that much was clear. That night, Josh finally moved out of my condo and onto the floor of his recording studio, where he's been ever since.

The next day, I lay in bed, my face tear streaked, scrolling on an iPad, looking at Wikipedia. *Damn.* Abraham Lincoln had syphilis? Al Capone died from it? Oscar Wilde, Baudelaire, and now…Bobbie Brown? I made the mistake of doing a Google Images search, and *FUUUUCK.* I gasped in horror at the bodies covered with reddish nodules. Facial deformations. Pustules colonizing people's crotches. This was my nightmare come true. The first stage of syphilis lasts one month. So does the second stage, and by the time you hit stage three, it's supposedly incurable. Blindness. Delirium. Then it eats your nose.

Josh called, delighted to report that he'd just gotten his test results back and they were *negative.* "I knew it, you're a whore, Bobbie Brown," he yelled.

I didn't believe him. He'd lied to me so many times over the years—about his porn addiction, the dick pics— and now I was supposed to believe that I'd magically contracted this disease from thin air? I was so distressed that week I suffered not one but two panic attacks so intense I was convinced they were heart attacks and that landed me in the emergency room. But there were no heart attacks. I was just freaking the fuck out, cursing the universe for playing yet another cruel joke on my ass.

My doctor sent me to a specialist who took further blood tests. Because I didn't have health insurance, I had to borrow the money to pay for my treatment, putting me further in the hole. Upon receiving the results, the doctor called me into his office. I panicked about what was coming: "Sorry, Bobbie, you're stage four. In a few weeks you'll have a mushroom for a vagina."

"Well, I must say, you've certainly been through the mill for somebody who's never had syphilis," the specialist said, looking up from his papers.

I choked a little. "Excuse me?"

"Yes, Bobbie. Whoever gave you the original test result got it wrong. You've never had syphilis."

I called those bastards at *Botched* and gave them a piece of my mind. Their response was along the lines of "oops, sorry!" I felt so guilty for what I had said to Josh, how I had accused him of lying to me. Somehow in my deluded, needy mind, I thought we'd be able to start over, to put all of this bad luck behind us. But Josh didn't want to. He didn't want to be glued to the arm of It Girl on Crutches, Bobbie Jean Brown. He wanted to move on, and in some ways, I was jealous. I wished I could figure out how to do the same.

WHY DO THE CHILDREN PLAY?

IT'S A GIDDY FEELING, waking up one morning and realizing you don't hate yourself. At least, not as much as you did yesterday. But that's how I felt when I found comedy, which brought with it a whole new way to view the chaos, the mistakes, and the heartbreaks of my life. Finally, they served a purpose. I no longer judged myself with cruel, ageist eyes—now, I saw my life's wobbly missteps as necessary calamities along the road to funny. All that baggage had turned into material, and the most disappointing aspects of my life story were now primo fodder for my newly minted stage persona: Miss Bobbie Jean Brown, oldest new kid on the Comedy Strip.

Now, I just had to figure out how to pay for the classes with Jimmy. So I did what all starving artists do best and I called Mom. I pitched her my plan to study with Jimmy until I was the sharpest, sassiest, most hilarious blonde this side of the Mississippi. No more watching some guy noodle his Fender from the side of the stage. This time, the spotlight was mine. As a consummate stage mom who'd sent me to etiquette and modeling classes from the age of seven to my teenage years, my mom needed very little persuading. She gave me her credit card information, and her blessing.

"I've got a good feeling about this one, Bob," she said.

Her investment paid off fast, and within three weeks of starting classes with Jimmy, I had performed two headline shows, both times blacking out and floating away like a birthday balloon. By the time my third show rolled around, I was determined to take back control. I wanted to actually be there, to witness the Bobbie Brown Comeback Experience firsthand instead of hearing about it from my friends and teacher afterward.

Backstage before my third show, I tried to relax my mind, calm my breath. *In through the nose, out through the mouth.* Every so often, my inner saboteur would interrupt my meditation. *They only want you here because you're the Cherry Pie Girl. You're just an extension of Tommy Lee's dick.*

Whenever those negative thoughts came swarming, I swatted them away like flies. Nope. Not tonight. No more of that. People had always put me in a box labeled girlfriend/wife/sex object/whore. And to some degree, I'd been content to remain in that box. But those labels stopped working for me a long time ago—if I wanted the world to see me as more than just the Cherry Pie Girl, I'd have to stand up and show them why.

I strode across the stage, took the mic, and began my set.

So my gynecologist asked me today if I was sexually active. I had to say yes, because life fucks me on the regular. Then she asked me what form of birth control I've been using. I said, "My personality." Truth is, I've reached a point in my life where I've had to ask myself what the fuck went wrong. 'Cause Prince Charming isn't coming for me on a white horse. He's on a turtle somewhere, lost and confused, asking for directions. So the other day I said fuck it. I have the worst luck dating, might as well just go out and have sex with the first man I see.

With the room's full attention, I launched into a strange, imagined scenario of casual, consensual sex in which, beat by beat, I systematically dismantled the notion of Bobbie Brown as an object of desire.

So I grab this guy and he says, "Give me a blow job." And because I'm not a quitter, I say, "Okay." I'm pretty sure I can smell his ass and it's bad, real bad. Something's happening though. He's jerking, he's twerking, he's screaming loud as fuck, he's flailing all over the place. I'm fucking great at this! I'm the fucking best. Somebody should be fucking filming me right now. I should probably get a trophy for this. I need an award! I'm the shit. I'm fucking great. Oh, wait. He's not enjoying this—he's having a seizure.

I looked at the audience. They were loving it...loving *me*, dare I say. It didn't seem to matter how weird or gross or unsexy I got, they were lapping it up. This fake story was the realest I'd ever been. And I was there. Present. Feeling it, living it, loving it, commanding the stage, raining down joke after joke, making them squirm, making them *mine*.

This is the most incredible feeling! I thought, under-standing my musician exes more than ever before. This is why they ride in freezing tour buses for months on end, playing songs on tiny stages in shitty bars. Being yourself and *actually being loved for it* is a high better than any other drug.

Right at the end of my set, Jimmy walked on stage holding a cake illuminated by dozens of flickering candles. It was my forty-ninth birthday, and the whole room clapped and cheered as I blew out the candles. *This is the best birthday of my fucking life,* I thought.

Walking into the backstage area, I heard someone calling my name; it was the big star of the night, actor and hot-stuff comedian Jamie Kennedy, who rose to fame in 1996 as Randy Meeks, the horror-movie geek in *Scream*.

"You were really funny!" Jamie said, warmly. "Really, really good."

I'd heard that comedians can be competitive and unsupportive, but tonight I felt nothing but love.

"Happy birthday!" he continued. "How old are you, anyway?"

"Forty-nine and feeling fine," I said.

"Oh, my God, shut up. Do you ever age, Bobbie Brown?"

"Nah, ask my dermatologist. She accepts food stamps, by the way."

"Whatever you're doing, it's working," he said. "Bring it in, old lady."

Then he hugged me. Like, the extra-long type of hug.

"By the way, that blowjob joke was amazing," he said. "I was totally in that scene with you. I can't believe he had a seizure!"

"Oh, those jokes aren't real," I explained. "There's no way I would actually pick up a guy off the street and give him a blowjob."

"Oh, so I shouldn't believe what you say?" he said.

"Not all of it."

"Good! 'Cause I was starting to worry about your safety."

"You're not the first, honey," I said. "You're not the first."

When Jamie took the stage, he talked about me for five minutes straight. "Bobbie was great, wasn't she? She and I grew up in the same era. Back then, Bobbie Brown was the hottest thing in Hollywood. I mean, *I* certainly wouldn't look that good in a Warrant video." Listening to him, a lightbulb lit up. *I should date a comedian!* I pictured a lifetime of funny where loading the dishwasher would be totally hilarious, going to the DMV would be a gigglefest, every day a series of side-splitting LOLs and pranks. Yes, wouldn't it be cool to live Funnily Ever After with someone? How had I never thought of this before?

With Jamie Kennedy still singing my praises onstage, I walked up to Jimmy and whispered loudly in his ear. "Do you think he's trying to...you know?"

Jimmy looked at me. "Do I think he's trying to fuck you? Who cares, Bobbie? So long as he wants to work with you again, that's all that matters."

"Right. Got it," I said. "But do you think—"

"Bobbie, just keep it professional."

Of course, the second I got home, I looked up Jamie on social media. I wanted to know more about my future comedy husband. A quick Google search revealed a string of beautiful, famous, and troublingly brunette ex-girlfriends, including Jennifer Love Hewitt, all of whom boasted thigh gaps far more substantial than mine. *Shit.* Next stop: Instagram. There he was. One hundred and sixteen thousand followers. I wondered if he'd notice me among the dozens of follow requests he no doubt got every day. I looked for the "Follow" button and instead saw "Follow Back". Ah. He'd already added me. Excellent. Immediately, I slid into his DMs.

"Hey, thanks so much for having me open for you. It was only my third time on stage." Little bubbles danced on my phone screen as he wrote his response.

"Third time ever? That's crazy, Bobbie. You're ahead of the game."

We both knew that my "Cherry Pie" legacy had fast-tracked me onto that stage. But, like Jimmy, Jamie seemed to think I might actually have enough talent to stay up there.

A couple of days later, I got a message from a radio host in Philly I've known for some time. It was a photo of him and Jamie Kennedy waving. "Do you know Jamie? He says he knows you," read the message.

I typed back, excited. "Don't tell him, but I totally have a high school crush on him right now…"

"Do you want me to give him your number?" wrote my friend.

"Only if he asks for it."

The next day, Jamie sent me a text. "You got me now. Save my number."

SOUTHERN HARMONY

I T WAS SEVEN, THE morning after my wonderful birth-day show. My phone buzzed insistently on the bedside table. It had to be my mom. Only moms call at this hour.

"So, Bobbie how did it go last night?" she asked.

"I'm trying to sleep, Mom, gah."

Doesn't matter how old I get, I'm still 100 percent teenager whenever I talk to my mother. Bleary-eyed, I sent her some video clips from the show. I wasn't worried about how she'd react to the crude content—by now, she's well used to my potty mouth—but I did hope that she'd at least find me a little bit funny. I desperately needed her to believe in what I was doing. After all the years she'd spent worrying about me—what with Josh, the near-fatal car accident, the fall down the stairs—I owed her something that felt like hope.

She watched the videos and called me back. "You look very beautiful," she said. I waited, wondering if she'd enjoyed anything beside my looks.

"And you're very, very funny," she said.

My heart leapt with joy.

"Bobbie, my sweet baby," she continued. "Do you know how hard it is to reinvent yourself? Well, you've made it look easy. You know why? Because you're good." She was gushing, and it caught me off-guard, how proud she sounded.

This was a new development in our relationship, my mom approving of my life choices. I thanked her for believing in me—it had been a really long time since I'd given her a reason to. And I told her I owed it all to her.

"Oh, don't give me too much credit," she said. "You're pretty much self-taught."

I was starting to tear up; it was way too early for this much emotion. I had to hang up the phone.

✳✳✳

MY MOM'S FULL NAME is Judy Ann Brown, and she's a Priscilla Presley lookalike who was born into a Catholic family in Church Point, Louisiana, the Cajun Music Capital of the World. It was a poor town; nearly one third of the families there lived below the poverty line. Mom used to talk about how horse-drawn carriages clip-clopped around town right up until the 1950s. She was the sixth of eight kids and had six brothers and a sister. She was sickly and all but bald for the first five years of her life. She was such a weird-looking kid that my grandma Isabelle made her wear a necklace dipped in holy water so Jesus would help her get prettier. Heaven must have listened because my mother grew up to be one fine-looking teenager.

But still, life was hard. My grandpa had walked out on the family when they were small, so my grandma had to raise the eight of them by herself. With such a large family, the children had to grow up fast. My mom was working long before she was legally old enough. There was simply no other way for them to make ends meet. Then, when she was seventeen, along came my dad: Bobby Gene Brown, a blue-eyed, Johnny Cash–type from the wrong side of the tracks. He always showed up at the house with groceries for the refrigerator, and my grandma liked that.

Bobby Gene played guitar, smelled of aftershave and Winstons, and wanted to be a country singer. He was born and raised in Spartanburg, South Carolina, a picturesque small town founded by French fur trappers. Think apple orchards, sleepy church spires, and men who express their feelings with their fists. His dad beat his wife—Bobby Gene's mom—badly, and one day, as a result, she suffered a brain hemorrhage and died. My dad, then a teenager, came home from school and found her. Ill-equipped to handle the tragedy, Bobby Gene ran away from his feelings by joining the military straight out of school and serving in Vietnam. When he came back, he moved down to Baton Rouge, became a car salesman, and drank away his dark memories from the war and the images of his father beating his mother to a pulp. Yet somehow, he managed to talk a good Catholic girl named Judy into marrying him. She was twenty years old when she gave birth to me, on October 7, 1969, and my dad insisted on calling me Bobbie Jean Brown, after himself.

I can't remember the first time I saw them fight, but I do have memories of my dad kicking my mom as she lay on the floor, and me screaming and screaming until he stopped. That's when I figured it out—that if I made enough noise, danced and sang and laughed loud enough to distract him, he'd snap out of his rage. So I'd do things like pour ketchup on my stomach and play dead—*over here, daddy!*—just to make it stop.

The older I got, the more I talked back, cursed, and got involved in the fights. Daddy would pick out a belt from the closet or a switch from a tree in the backyard and spank me. I'd bite my lip, fight back the tears, and smile bitterly through the stinging pain just to show him he couldn't hurt me. Just to have the last word. If I didn't cry, that meant I had won.

When I was in ninth grade, my mom finally decided to leave. It was over. No more fights. No more yelling. No more nights spent driving around the local bars, where we'd find my dad talking to some other woman. All that was behind us. I watched my mom reinvent herself, rebuild her whole life from scratch. My mother showed me that it's never too late to change your life completely. To lift yourself from the depths. For my mom, marriage had been a violent, degrading shit show, so everything from that point on would be the opposite. She would be the perfectly poised Southern Belle mother to her perfectly poised Southern Belle daughter.

At least, that was the plan.

She put my hair in curlers at night and drove me to New Orleans for white gloves, party manners classes, ballet, pageants, and dance competitions. Etiquette brought structure, status, and grace to our lives. External appearances were things we could polish and refine until they outshone the tatty, uncouth truths about our past. So nobody ever suspected we were broke because my mom managed to dress me beautifully with what little we had.

"You're a real pretty girl," Mom told me over and over, and I'd shrug, not quite believing her, not quite understanding why she needed everything to be so perfect, beautiful, and serene.

When one day she entered me into a pageant, I went along with it for her. I thought it was silly how competitive the other girls were, how bent out of shape they'd get about being pretty, being perfect. And then when I won, I remember feeling mildly surprised; I was mainly glad that Mom was finally happy. It seemed to inject her with new life. She said I should become a model, and I thought maybe that would be cool, especially if it helped me meet cute boys who wore makeup. That was *my* passion. I was crazy for the hair metal guys. Posters of Tommy Lee, my first crush and future love, were plastered all over my bedroom walls when I was a teenager.

After placing second runner-up in the Miss Teen USA contest, I received offers from modeling agencies, and that's how I moved to LA at age nineteen. I didn't have long-term goals back then; I didn't need to because things just seemed to happen for me without much effort on my part. The wind always seemed to blow me in the right direction since I was young, easy on the eyes, and fun to be around.

I soon became that blithe, entitled model/actress who gets calls for bookings worth thousands of dollars, yawns and says, "I'm too tired." When Steven Spielberg invited me to audition for the part of Tinkerbell in *Hook*, I canceled my audition no fewer than four different times because I was hungover. When I did eventually show up, I was drunk and kept spinning around in the office chair.

Steven stared at me in disbelief. "Bobbie, I want you to know I'm not giving you this part."

"Oh." I stopped spinning in the chair. "Well, why am I here?"

"Because I wanted to meet the person who no-showed on me four times. You need to get your shit together, lady."

I wish I'd listened to Steven Spielberg. So does my mom. Things might have worked out very differently if I'd taken the golden tickets being constantly dangled in front of me.

My mom chided me for partying so much, but what did she know? I liked having fun. Fun was how I got to be myself, be a kid again, reclaim my childhood. But at some point, my inner child began taking over. It seemed like I couldn't stop having fun even if I wanted to. Fun would seek me out, stalk me, follow me home long after I'd had my fill. I would walk into a club; the owner would shake my hand and press a bag of coke into my palm. If I booked a fashion campaign, my modeling agent would give me speed to help me drop five pounds before the shoot. I could have said no, but I didn't know how. Soon, my life was nothing but fun, and it was killing me. I had to get out. Leave Hollywood altogether. So in the early 2000s, I turned my back on the clubs and the parties, and I ran for my life. It was time to move back home.

"By the way, Subway's hiring," my mom told me in the car on the way home from the Baton Rouge airport the day I moved back.

I screamed, and started kicking the windshield, filled with shame and self-loathing. Why was she rubbing salt in my wounds? Was she angry at me for fucking up all of our beautiful dreams? Was she angry because when it came down to it, I was just like my dad?

***

BEING BACK IN BATON Rouge was a surreal rebirth that felt like a major step backward. Not knowing what else to do, I signed up for beauty school. When people recognized me in the corridors and asked me why I was there, I had trouble answering. What could I say without sounding like an asshole? That I was taking a vacation from fame? That I wasn't strong enough to make it?

"Just tell them the truth," my dad said. "Tell them you came home to spend time with your family."

You see, he accepted me when no one else did. Bobby Gene understood that addiction is a disease that makes devils of us all. Bobby Gene was the only adult in my life who didn't judge me because he knew what it felt like to be this lost, to feel ashamed and guilty for hurting the people you love most.

Those months in Baton Rouge, I'd often find myself on his doorstep, sobbing. And he'd take me in without a word and hug me until the tears stopped. Sometimes he'd play his guitar.

"Bobbie…I'm gonna show you how to play the blues," he said, smiling at me.

Being at my dad's, listening to him talk, sing, and strum, I could forget the sad feelings for a while.

This Southern outlaw, ex-military, country-music-loving alcoholic had beaten his wife and was once a walking cliché of toxic masculinity. But he had spent many years looking at himself in the mirror, trying to understand where his anger came from. And now, he wanted to help me do the same. He had become a different man. A man I was proud of. A man who had found Jesus, and who tried to show love to all those who were rejected and scorned by society.

I was spending a lot of time with my dad, cooking him dinner on the weekends. One day, I noticed he wasn't eating as much as he used to. He had lost weight, though he didn't seem to mind. In fact, he liked his trim figure and gave me money to buy him a whole new wardrobe. But something wasn't right. I made him go to the doctor, who ran some tests. For weeks, my dad pretended he was fine, even though his appetite had completely disappeared and he was throwing up every meal he tried to eat. Very quickly, as often happens with cancer, my strong and complicated father found that his body was no longer his friend. He faded away before my eyes, but denying he was sick until the very end. He passed away just before dawn one night, holding my brother's hand, singing an old hymn, "I've Found a Friend in Jesus."

Memories of my dad's kind, unjudging soul lingered on every street corner in Baton Rouge. It was too painful for me to be there with him gone, so I told my mom I was going back to LA and taking my daughter with me.

Something shifted in me after my father's death. It reassembled my priorities and reminded me that I had to walk my own path. I couldn't do that in Baton Rouge.

"Well, all I'll say is I hope you're not getting back into entertainment," my mom said coldly.

***

THE ATMOSPHERE BETWEEN ME and my mother remained hostile for years. We were stuck in a loop—she'd lambast my life choices, I'd hate her lack of faith in me, and we'd scream about it. Rinse and repeat. For years, we were at war, deep in the trenches of an anger dug over decades. A couple of years ago, I noticed her anger take an interesting turn. It wasn't just me she was getting mad at; it was anyone who stepped in her way.

One day, in Baton Rouge, she began screaming at a group of teenage boys in the street for no apparent reason. "Fuck you, you little fucking shits!" she yelled.

"Fuck you, bitch!" one of the boys yelled back. My mom dropped her shopping bags and raised her fists in the air.

"Why don't you come over here and say that to my face, fucker!"

Wow. Judy had gone full fucking gangster.

"Sorry, fellas, she drinks…ignore her," I said, trying to placate the kids.

"I DON'T DRINK AND I NEVER HAVE!" screamed my street-fighter mom.

I dragged her back to the car in order to avoid a gang fight.

"What the hell was that all about?" I asked her.

"Go fuck yourself, Bobbie."

My mom had always had a sharp tongue, but this language was really out of character.

Turned out, there was a reason for my mother's personality change: years of fried chicken, cakes, and sweets had clogged her carotid artery, and a lack of oxygen to the brain can have the curious side effect of transforming Martha Stewart into Satan. A surgery removed the blockage and soon afterward, with fresh oxygen pumping into her brain, she remembered her old self. No more fights with strangers. Just fights with me. Always with me.

She came to Los Angeles to visit my brother's baby, and I noticed she'd lost a lot of weight. My brother thought she had an eating disorder, but at sixty-five, with a lifetime of baking and deep frying behind her, anorexia seemed unlikely. All I could think about was what happened when my dad got sick. The loss of meat from his bones. The sunken cheeks. The sickening realization that I had taken this person for granted for so many years. If my mom got sick, it would fall on me to become the matriarch of our family and be the anchor for Taylar and myself. The thought was so overwhelming. I wasn't sure I was strong enough to be that person. I'm still not.

I begged my mom to go to the doctor. "Okay, okay," she said, reluctant to put herself through more tests. The day of her appointment, I was a nervous wreck. I felt waves of guilt, thinking back on all the fights we'd had, the stress I'd put her through over the years. How it must have felt, watching me unravel time and time again while she raised my daughter. After all that she'd been through with my father. I promised I would never take her for granted again. Just please, God, let her be okay.

Then, a photo of something horrible popped up on my phone. A fleshy black hole. It was my mom's esophagus. She'd been losing blood for at least a year. The only option was surgery, but my mom refused. She said she felt too weak.

"Tell me what my mother should do," I asked a psychic that afternoon, offering him no other information.

He frowned. "Something needs to be addressed, and quickly. In the next two weeks. Otherwise, it's going to be bad."

I called my mom immediately. "You have to get the surgery! Please, Mom, I'm begging you…" I don't think she'd ever heard me so upset. Within a day, my mom had scheduled the surgery. She's been recuperating, step by step, ever since.

"You matter so much to me, Mom, I wish you'd take better care of yourself," I told her, after the operation. The irony was not lost on Judy.

"Yes, I wish you'd take better care of yourself, too, Bobbie."

After that, something shifted between us. We started having the talks we never had. About life. About the mistakes we'd both made. About how, for all our differences, we're so very similar. Finally, the storm that had raged between my mother and myself for so many years began to subside. That's the strange gift of illness in the family, I suppose. Even death has a hidden light that, if allowed to turn on, can provide wisdom and remind you to take care of everyone whom you love. Including your parents.

STAY GOLD

JOSH, MY EX, CAME over unannounced, and not for the first time.

"I'm busy," I said, standing on the doorstep.

"Oh, you're busy?" Josh gave me that look. He knew I was weak, that I hadn't quite gotten over my taste for things that are bad for me. So he kept trying, over and over. It was just a game to him, one he'd won many times before.

"I'm trying to write my comedy set. Leave me alone," I said.

He nodded. "Sure, babe. I'll come by another time."

He kept sniffing around, a stray cat looking for scraps. Well, guess what: kitchen's closed. I'd been down that road too often, and each time, it took me somewhere painful. I would just erase him from my life entirely if I could, but he always found a way to reach me. He was cunning, with multiple identities on social media. If I blocked him, he simply opened a new account and messaged me from that one, carrying on the conversation as though nothing had happened.

"Baby, if you want me to come over, just say so."

"Baby, are you hungry?"

"Baby, let me in."

He wanted me—at least for the night—and then he'd slink away. That was probably how it should always have been between us; some people are never meant to be more than overnight visitors.

My family knew that about Josh the second they met him. They couldn't believe I had fallen for the first guy I matched with on Tinder. My stepdad William Willamson told him, "I hope you know you'll never be worthy of her, son." And my mom asked him if he required a babysitter.

But Taylar was the meanest.

The first words she said to him were "you're not my father." Her Christmas presents to him were always interesting: a bag of dirt one year ("'cause he's a dirt bag, Mom..."), a gay porn paperback called *Pounded in the Butt by My Own Butt* another year. When she learned he'd been sending dick pics all over town, Taylar declared war.

Well, I guess I'm going to have to hunt you down and punch your dick off now. Maybe not today, maybe not tomorrow, but one day when you least expect it, I am going to find you and it's going to happen.

Taylar sent that text message to Josh followed by a groin protector cup, which she sent to him in the mail.

When we finally broke up, following the syphilis-that-never-was incident, Taylar took the opportunity to remind him exactly what she thought of him.

Dear Josh,

Now that you and my mom are broken up and you finally pushed her too far, I feel that I can express myself freely. You might as well do yourself a favor, stop delaying the inevitable, and move back to the ol' homestead on a farm in the middle of bumfuck nowhere, where you can fulfill your destiny of rapidly fading into obscurity. It'll probably be less embarrassing moving home now as opposed to when you're forty and still haven't accomplished anything and have nothing to show for yourself. Why waste any more time? I'm sure you can find some young girl to abuse emotionally and send unimpressive dick pics to.... You think you're hot shit, but you're repugnant. You think you're tough, but you're a coward. You think you're smart, but I'm smarter. You think you're mean. I'm meaner.

Wow. Taylar has always had a way with words. Ironically, I think she got through to Josh in a way that I never could because quite soon after she sent him that message, he started his own business.

✳✳✳

DURING ONE OF THE last fights Jani and I ever had, he broke his guitar over the coffee table in our house in Tarzana, yelling, "I'm not the man in this family!"

It's a perplexing attitude, the idea that men and women should act a certain way in relationships. I think there are leaders and there are followers and whether you're a man or a woman is beside the point. I tend to lead in relationships because I have a very strong personality, but that doesn't make me a man. It makes me Bobbie.

Jani didn't like it, but he wasn't strong enough to tame me. Tommy came close, until I rebelled, and he watched in horror as his perfect almost-wifey Bobbie turned into a maniacal zombie, a skeletal drug fiend clawing at the walls and hell-bent on escape. Some caged animals bite back, you see…

I don't want to be in the driving seat anymore, as I was with Josh and Jani. And I don't want to be a passenger either, like I was with Tommy. I want something in the middle. Someone grounded and mature enough to hold his own, but free-spirited and up for adventure. My only chance of finding that, I think, is to date people closer to my own age—uncharted territory for me, since I've never in my life loved anyone over the age of thirty-four. Tommy was thirty-four when we split. So was Josh. Jani was twenty-seven when we divorced. In all my years of dating, I've yet to experience a relationship with anyone more than a year older than Jesus was on the cross. For some reason, the hot silver foxes of the world, the men of means and looks, have always been invisible to me.

A famous French author was once chastised online for saying he could never be attracted to a fifty-year-old body. Honestly, I agreed with him. (His body in particular was as appealing to me as a used dog poop bag floating down the LA River.) This is why I was never able to sleep with the Rod Stewarts of the world; despite their wealth, flair, and confidence, all I could think was "how low do those

things actually hang?" Hot, young guys with an edge—
that's always been my type—much like the fifty-something
French author who's happiest being naked with women
who are twenty-five and preferably Asian.

When we were in our twenties, some of my friends preferred the company of older men and would quite happily
have dated that middle-aged Frenchman. They enjoyed older guys' savoir faire, the quality of their conversation, their
understanding of human relationships. The money helped
too. But my brain has always operated more like a man's.
For me, a firm body trumps a full wallet. A pretty face star-
ing adoringly at mine is more appealing than a wise mind.

I've tended to judge men over forty as harshly as I'm
sure they now judge me, and I'm paying the price. Most
days I'm knee deep in romantic overtures from men in
their twenties who start love letters with, "Is your ass still
hot?" This usually leads into, "Kinda sorta wish you were
choking on my dick right now," which I suppose is sweeter
than some of the messages I receive from women, who are
like, "AREN'T YOU THAT WHORE WHO COULDN'T
TAKE CARE OF HER KID?"

And that's just on social media.

Every time I'm bored enough to venture onto Tinder,
Bumble, or Hinge, it's a shit show. For instance:

"I hope you like barbecues, because I'm gonna slap
this meat across your grill."

"I like my breakfast sausage blown."

"Hey, do you like my belt buckle? It would look better
against your forehead!"

"I'd like roses on my casket after you murder this dick."

Yes, those are some of the actual, real messages I have received.

Not long ago I accidentally swiped right on a young guy who convinced me to give him my number so that we could text. But then he had the audacity to call me on the phone instead—which, today, is the equivalent of showing up at somebody's front door naked.

"Why are you calling me?" I asked him.

"Because you didn't respond to my text."

"So?"

"Aw, you're a shy cookie, aren't you?"

"I'm not a shy cookie. I'm a busy cookie, child. Goodbye."

I wished I could rent a billboard over the Sunset Strip reading "Bobbie Brown No Longer Dates Millennials." I wanted Josh to see it. I wanted him to know the game was pointless, him coming 'round here, giving me those eyes. Because the days of Bobbie Brown riding that young pony are over.

NOT FOR A MILLION DOLLARS

I WAS AT A pizza parlor in Silver Lake with Sharise Neil and our mutual gal pal Gretchen Bonaduce. Sugar, spice, and all things nice, we are the two-thirds-blonde-and-a-third-red, Powerpuff alumna of the Sunset Strip. We even have the battle scars to prove it. The three of us know all of each other's secrets and our most life-changing mistakes, and love nothing more than talking about them.

I've known Sharise for thirty years. We clicked the second we met, talked nonstop without taking a breath, and immediately became the type of best friends who called each other five times a day, and still do. Those are the special friendships, the ones that only come along a few times in a lifetime. They're rare, and what's even more surprising is when they last. We've bonded through friendship, motherhood, and divorces from cheating rock star husbands—truly, the best foundation for a friendship.

She's still the same slim, perfectly-toned, perfectly-poised, former mud wrestler I knew when she was married to Mötley Crüe singer Vince Neil, the guy who rubbed egg burritos on his crotch to hide the smell of other women. The guy who once told a journalist "our only regret is we can't eat all the pussy we see here tonight." The guy who… well, you get the picture. They were together from 1987 to 1993, and I met her in 1992, when things were seriously unraveling. Vince was spiraling into lethally reckless behavior, infidelities, and addictions that consumed whatever semblance of love still existed between them.

Whenever I heard anything questionable about Vince's behavior from Jani, even if it meant betraying Jani's confidence, I'd make sure to let Sharise know by using our special girl code. If she asked me a question and I said, "I don't know," the answer was yes. Things came to a head when Vince smashed his Ford Pantera into another car in Redondo Beach, California, killing his passenger, Hanoi Rocks drummer Nick "Razzle" Dingley. Even though Vince threatened to cut her off financially if she left, Sharise knew it would be safer for her and her daughter, Skylar, to start over.

Skylar and Taylar were around the same age and were best friends too. Those were the good times, the four of us together, every day. When Skylar was diagnosed with Wilms' tumor, a rare kidney cancer that only affects children, she underwent six operations, chemotherapy, and radiation treatments. But the treatments didn't work and four months after her diagnosis, on August 15, 1995, little Skylar passed away. I was in Louisiana at the time, and after Vince, I was the first person Sharise called. As soon as I hung up the phone, I got on the next flight out of there and showed up at her house with a suitcase. I stayed with her for two months, sleeping in her bed so she didn't have to be alone while she cried tears no mother should ever have to shed. Sharise and I have been to hell and back together, and our friendship, at this point, deserves a lifetime achievement award.

Gretchen, while a much newer friend to me than Sharise, is also a "sister from another mister." She too has a failed showbiz marriage in her past, having been married to Danny Bonaduce, the *Partridge Family* child star, whom she wed on November 4, 1990—the same day they met on a blind date. Danny may not have been a rock star, but he certainly partied like one, as shown on *Breaking Bonaduce,* the reality show about their marriage that ran from 2005 to 2006. When Gretchen saw her husband's infidelities, Napoleon complex, and addiction to steroids paraded for the whole world to see on the small screen, she finally set aside her "stand by your man" principles and packed her bags.

As we munched on pepperoni pizza, Sharise gave us the dirt on her latest Bumble flirtation. She'd gotten back on the app since the flames of love she'd felt for her firefighter boyfriend had been suddenly put out. They'd been dating a year and a half, never fought, had gone on three vacations, said "I love you," the whole shebang. A few nights after deciding to move in together, the firefighter said something that didn't ring true and Sharise's spidey sense compelled her to look at his phone while he was in the bathroom, something she'd never done before. Turned out, her bullshit radar was on point—she found messages between him and a woman he'd gone on a date with the night before. She didn't say anything to him. Instead, she quietly gathered her things, brushed her hair, put on lipstick, and kissed him goodbye. Forever.

When she got home, she called the girl, whose number she'd saved. "Hello, my name is Sharise. Quick question for you: did you happen to go on a date with a firefighter called Steve the other night?"

"Why, yes, we've been talking for a couple of weeks."

"Okay, great, thank you for verifying that. Well, I suppose I ought to let you know that he's my boyfriend; we've been together for a year and half. There's nothing wrong with our relationship. In fact, we just had sex. But if you want him you can have him." *Boom.* Sharise never spoke to the cheating firefighter again. Back to Bumble it was.

She told us about a cute guy in his forties with whom she'd been going back and forth on Bumble for weeks. They'd shared information about their lives, their marriages, their divorces. Small steps toward something that felt like intimacy. Then, after several conversations, he ghosted. "I wish he'd told me that threesomes were required before I got, you know, hopeful," Sharise said, wistfully.

"Regular threesomes are a fundamental need for this guy?"

"Yes," she said. "He and his ex-wife had an open relationship where they could hook up with men and women, go on threesome retreats, and—"

"Wait, *threesome retreats*?"

"Yeah, wife-swapping and husband-swapping in spa hotels, that kind of thing. I told him I wasn't into that kind of dating. And that was it. Over. Hard ghost."

I had a three-way once, in the late eighties, on the brown, carpeted living room floor of the Hollywood apartment I shared with my Chippendale boyfriend, Steve. One night he brought home a lesbian called Brandi, and I did my sporting best to enjoy myself, even though I'm not attracted to women. That night Steve got Brandi pregnant and since then—call me an out-of-touch monogamous traditionalist—I've steered clear of any scenario involving more than two sets of private parts. All that Fifty Shades of Eyes Wide Shut stuff, passing your genitalia around like cupcakes—fine if you're into it, but not my cup of tea.

I wondered if our inability to embrace the polyamorous lifestyle was the thing holding us back from finding The One. Maybe there is no The One, maybe there's The Two. Or The Twelve. Is true love the sum of its (many) parts? I would like to grow old with someone, buy matching walkers, go on cruises to Norway, and hang out at trivia nights in the Valley. But instead of looking for one retirement buddy, would I be better off dating the entire retirement home?

We decided to consult the Predict A Pen, a fun little toy that Gretchen had bought me for my birthday. You ask it a question, click the top, and it reaches into the future to find answers. "Dare you live by the pen?" the packaging asked.

Dare accepted, said Sharise, who went first.

"Will I find the love of my life—even though I don't want to go on a threesome retreat?" she said, clicking the end of the pen.

"HELL YEAH," came the response. A fine verdict.

Sharise handed the pen to me. I tried to think of a good question to ask. I knew I was never going to be happy sharing my lover with anyone else; I'd want him all to myself. The question was, who? I closed my eyes and blurted out the first thing that came to mind.

"Does Jamie Kennedy like me?"

Sharise clapped her hands. She's convinced I'll find my next soul mate in comedy. My own personal (monogamous) chucklefucker.

"IT'S UNCLEAR, ASK AGAIN."

I clicked again.

"IF YOU'RE LUCKY."

Defective piece of shit. I clicked again.

"NOT FOR A MILLION DOLLARS."

"The pen has spoken," I said, handing it to Gretchen.

Unlike Sharise and me, Gretchen's sorted on the relationship front; she's happily in love with a six-foot-five drummer. Her career was in a good place too; she'd just published her memoir and sings in a killer tribute band called The Fatal 80s. Her problem was that she hates LA. "How are my kids ever going to afford rent in this damn town?" she sighed, and I knew exactly what she meant. There's a Winnebago on every corner in LA with people inside who can't afford to pay rent because they got one parking ticket that doubled that turned into a court appearance that turned into their car getting impounded and then a bench warrant and jail. "Justice" in this town has become a way for the city of Los Angeles to finance itself through hefty and unreasonable fines placed on poor people for the most minor and mundane of infractions. Now, me, I'm attracted to abusive situations, which is why I still love living in LA no matter how inhumane it has become. When the big earthquake happens, you'll see me sitting on the rubble, cracking jokes with the cockroaches. But Gretchen wants out. She wants to live in Arizona, in a nice big house, surrounded by endless blue skies and horses.

Thus, her question for the Predict A Pen:

"Will I sell my house?"

"DUDE, NO WAY," said the pen.

I breathed a sigh of relief. I didn't want her to leave, ever. She's generous, appreciative, and always encouraging me to push forward with my career, to focus on myself instead of the relationships that always seem to consume me. Her and Sharise, they're the closest thing I have to family in LA.

For some time, Gretchen had been urging me to get moving on a follow-up to my book *Dirty Rocker Boys*. That book came out in 2013, and a lot had happened since then—most importantly, my new adventure in comedy. "I'm going to put you in touch with my publisher," said Gretchen.

"What if they say no?" I fretted. It's not easy getting a book deal in this day and age.

"Why don't we see what the Predict A Pen says?" said Sharise, handing it to me. I took it and closed my eyes.

"Will I publish a book, become an accomplished stand-up comedian, and find love with an age-appropriate man?"

I hit the button. Nothing happened. I hit it again. And again. Sharise and Gretchen looked at one another. The Predict A Pen had jammed.

RUNNING IN FLIP-FLOPS

I FELT MY CELL phone buzz in my jeans back pocket. It was an email from my landlord wishing me a happy Friday, and that oh, by the way, he wanted to inform me that he'd be doubling my rent "in accordance with market values," giving me sixty days to tell him whether I would accept his rent hike or give up my lease and get out. The horror of the unjust LA rental market was no longer a scary thing that happened to other people. It was now my reality.

I looked around on the rental sites and what I saw made me want to cry. A nice, grown-up one bedroom in LA with a yard and parking averages $2,200 a month. Besides, I didn't want to leave my place, not now. I liked my house; I liked the quiet little suburb of Arleta; I liked having a place I could finally call home. I'm no hobo, no tramp steamer, no traveling circus tumbleweed. I'm tired of kicking the can, being a cockroach, popping up in every Goddamn neighborhood in LA—Westwood, Malibu,

Hollywood, West Hollywood, Los Feliz, Sherman Oaks, Studio City, Woodland Hills, Tarzana, Encino, North Hollywood. I'd lived everywhere, and I was done with it. I liked my house and my private, double garage. Leaving Arleta would mean facing the very real possibility of street parking—words that trigger a specific kind of PTSD for many of us in LA. Street parking means driving around for three hours a night before you find a spot. Street parking means waking up at 6:00 a.m. to avoid getting towed. If you park for longer than seventy-two hours and someone complains, street parking means a $500 ticket. When I lived in Hollywood in a street-parking-only situation, I got so many tickets my car ended up getting impounded. Every day is Mercury Retrograde when you have street parking. Street parking is Satan's work.

At the time I received the news about my rent increase I had two of my three bedrooms sublet out. One renter stayed in her room a lot but always paid her bills on time. The second was a man who moved in with just a bed, a desk, and a bottle of lotion. For the first two months, he never spent the night in his room. Then he went to Ibiza for a long while and didn't elaborate any further. I have never loved living with strangers, but I was grateful to have them because they helped me make my rent and retain access to my big, beautiful garage.

I sat down with the roomies and asked if they'd be willing to absorb the increased rent if we split it three ways. They both nodded. *Of course, Bobbie. We'll get through this together.* Relieved, I told my landlord we'd be staying on. I signed a new lease, and within weeks both of them changed their minds. The girl got a job in Vegas. And the guy, well, I guess he decided to spend more time in Ibiza. Now I was stuck with a fresh, unaffordable lease, no roommates, and no idea what I was going to do.

I sat at my desk, terrible visions floating through my head. A Winnebago with a "welcome home" mat. A mountain of parking tickets. Thread-bare couches provided by well-meaning friends. Looks of disappointment in my daughter's and mother's eyes when I told them that the rug had been pulled out from under me. Again.

Find the funny, Bobbie, I told myself. *It's all material, remember?*

✳✳✳

I STEPPED ONTO THE stage and looked out at the crowd of shadows before me, the welcome applause both uplifting and nauseating. The roller coaster ride was beginning again. I gripped the mic and smiled, happy that for almost twenty minutes I could totally forget today's bad news. Comedy is therapy, a temporary escape from reality, a guaranteed ego boost whatever the weather.

"Good evening. My name's Bobbie Brown, and I'm currently in a long-distance relationship with my boyfriend who lives in the future. I can't wait to meet him."

Chuckles.

"So, the last guy I talked to on a dating app said he lived in a gated community. Prison. He meant prison. Anyway, dating apps are so depressing, occasionally I'll consider getting back together with my millennial ex. Then I remember I'd rather shit in my hands and clap."

Laughter erupted, and endorphins flooded my body.

"I want a guy who's cute. Who knows what songs not to talk over. Who's good at sex. And by 'good at sex,' I mean, the kind of sex that sounds like you're running in flip-flops. The kind so good that even your neighbors need a cigarette after. Unfortunately, most times I have sex these days, guys will literally nut forty-five seconds into it and have the audacity to ask me, *did you come?* Fuck yeah, I came—to the wrong fucking house."

***

Two very cute girls came up to me asking for selfies after the show. They said they had flown in from China specifically to see me. CHINA. Seven thousand miles, just to see me. "Holy shit, that's fucking crazy!" I said, calling over Sharise and pointing at the girls proudly. "Check it out—CHINA!"

The second they got their selfie they disappeared.

"Okay, bye," they said, and shuffled away, trying to be polite. It was strange; I thought they'd at least want to talk some more. Were they in awe of me? I really had to know.

"Bobbie, stop. You don't need to be friends with your fans," said Sharise.

"Why not? I like them, and they like me," I said, wishing they would come back.

"Bobbie, I think your set's a little schtick-ish," Sharise said. She thought I should tell real stories about my own life instead of just the zany jokes about made-up dating scenarios. "I understand that going out there and being yourself is going to feel pretty raw, because if they reject your real self it might be too much for you to take," she continued. "But I think you should dig into your real relationships, with guys, with your mom. Talk about how she wanted you to be a beauty queen, but instead she got this beautiful girl who talks about pubes."

She was right. I didn't want to go there. And I didn't want to discuss why.

"Hey, Bobbie!" It was my teacher, Jimmy. "Good work, you kill it every time." I gave Sharise a look that said "see?"

"Just one thing," he added. "Stop writing a new set every time and expecting it to work. Because one day it won't. And trust me, there's nothing less sexy than bombing on stage."

"Here's what I think," I said, irritated with all the well-intentioned, unsolicited advice. "If it ain't, broke don't fix it."

He shrugged. "Your funeral, Bobbie."

So what if I wanted to reinvent the wheel every night? So what if I wanted people to come back and see me over and over again and never have to hear the same joke twice? I didn't want to fall back on the sad, embarrassing stories of my past. I wanted to stand on the edge of the precipice and jump off into the future. My kamikaze approach to comedy was strikingly similar to my approach to life. You either land on your feet or smash your face into a table at the bottom of the stairs. No in between. That's rock 'n' roll.

HORMONALLY YOURS

I WAS DELIRIOUS WITH stress. The pressure of turning a few one-off shows into a long-running comedy career was weighing on me along with my housing issues. Not to mention, I hadn't been laid since prehistory. I wasn't used to such long fallow periods, having generally preferred to have bad relationships with sex to no relationships with no sex.

Dangerous, self-destructive thoughts floated through my consciousness. *Josh…he's always DTF. What about the young guys on Tinder?* If only Jamie Kennedy would just pony up and ask me out on a date. Surely once you've texted more than thirty times it's all right to get naked? But he wasn't getting the hint. Only one option remained. I could shut my sex drive off altogether. Pull the plug on my blue balls. Come off the hormones I'd been taking to stave off the symptoms of menopause and let the dust finally begin to settle on my trusty four-poster bed…

Three years earlier, my lifelong desire to have penises inside me suddenly ceased. It was liberating yet confusing, because I had always been very amorous. Even my ex thought I was a freak. I was a sex ninja, a gold medalist in the love Olympics, the goddess of Mount Fuck. A well-oiled sex machine, the kind of lover who could instigate passionate "running in flip-flops" sex four times a day. Then, overnight, I turned into Miss Marple. *Get away from me with your...thing!* I thought, as Josh approached with that horny puppy dog look in his eyes. I didn't even want to fuck myself. As my collection of vibrators gathered dust, I wondered what was wrong with me and my dwindling sex drive. Was I consuming too many pesticides and GMOs? Were my concerns about global warming and animal cruelty finally spilling over into the bedroom? Of course not. Deep down, I knew *exactly* what was happening.

For a while, there was literally no more frightening word in the English language. *Men—oh, pause.* It reads exactly like the thing that it is. The thing that presses "pause" on your relationship with mankind. (Ignore this analogy if you're not sexually attracted to them.) All the things that had defined my entire identity thus far were put at risk when menopause entered the picture, from the teen beauty pageants to being a spokesmodel on *Star Search* to starring in all those hair metal music videos to my current MILF Empress status. My ideas of beauty and femininity were in disarray, and my craving to be desired by the opposite sex was about to go down the toilet, along with the last dregs of my hormones and an old slice of cherry pie.

I never lie about my age, even though I'm truly terrified of aging, and I struggle with the march of time every day. There is a school of thought that says women can and should age gracefully, embracing the various stages as they arrive, celebrating their deepening lines as evidence of a life well lived. But for a long time, I couldn't even bear to look in the mirror, so alarming were the little etchings on my skin. They felt like notches on a belt I couldn't take off. Luckily, in this day and age, there's help for people like me. My friends Botox and Juvederm (as administered by Oksana Fursevich, my trusty injectables doctor), La Mer, Bikram, Pilates, HIIT videos on YouTube, coconut oil, apple cider vinegar, charcoal toothpaste, homemade scrubs, yoni crystals, maca powder, turmeric, vampire facials, emotional support peacocks, butthole exfoliants, and, of course, Clarendon and Sienna—my favorite Instagram filters. These are all tools in the armory of hot, ageless women redefining what "older" looks like, and they are employed with varying degrees of grace. But what about the internal changes? How do we manage those?

I had heard about Bioidentical Hormones from friends who were also in the process of retiring their egg factories. Bioidenticals are an alternative to regular hormone replacement therapy made using yam and soybean extracts and are marketed as "more natural" and therefore safer than regular hormone therapy. They're controversial because some doctors think they're actually *more* carcinogenic than HRT. Who cares? All I know is that Oprah's a fan, and if Oprah's on board, so am I.

I went to see my doctor, Gayle Jackson, who's been my physician for nearly thirty years and who also delivered Taylar. She took a swab of my saliva and confirmed my hormonal shit show. Now I had to decide if I was going to start taking the hormones. There was a possibility of weight gain, the doctor warned me, and I personally knew someone who had gained forty pounds on bioidenticals. *Do I grow a bigger butt, or bring sexy back?* I pondered. Judge Judy reruns, elastic waistbands, and Candy Crush— those are the images that we've been fed about post-menopausal women, and that's not me. I'm still a teenager. I'm still figuring myself out. I'm not ready for the M-word, even if it thinks it's ready for me. In the end, it was an easy decision. I started shooting up yam-based bioidenticals and all of a sudden my hoo-ha had reopened for business. It was Black Friday down there, I'm telling you.

My first month of taking the hormones, I was so horny all I wanted to do was play guitar solos on my crotch all day long. *Now I understand what it feels like to be a man*, I thought, bringing myself to orgasm for the eighth time that day. It felt like I had just discovered my clitoris. Being on the hormones gave me a whole new perspective on the male condition. *No wonder they're pigs!* I marveled, lost in the throes of getting off all day, every day. *No wonder Josh had his dick in his hand all the time and sent photos of it to hundreds of girls who aren't his girlfriend! It's nature! It's beautiful!* When I was pumped full of hormones, sex became an itch that had to be scratched—no more, no less.

I had a friend whose wife had also lost interest in sex because of the changes brought about by menopause. He asked me if I could introduce him to women who might be interested in sleeping with him on the side.

"First, you're a fucking pig," I said with full sincerity but also sympathizing with him a little now that I'd had a taste of being a sex maniac. "Second, get your wife on Bioidenticals instead of destroying your family, you idiot."

It took a few months of tweaking the levels before my doctor and I found the perfect dosage of Bioidenticals for me. My sex drive settled back to normal, and the early signs of—squirm—menopause subsided. Strange thing was, even though I was able to have sex with Josh, I didn't really want to anymore. This wasn't because of my hormones or any kind of change of life. My body may have been going through menopause, but my heart was going through man-o-pause. I had to press pause on *him*.

GAME OVER

I HAD BLOCKED JOSH on all social media platforms after the last time he'd showed up on my doorstep unannounced. But we did have a prior arrangement for him to watch my dog while I went to Louisiana to visit my family. Nupa was the closest thing to a child we had, and she was very attached to both of us. And as mad as I was at him for all the shitty things that had transpired in our relationship, I figured if he wanted to honor our agreement, I would give him the opportunity.

"Hey," I wrote. "It's me. I know we haven't been able to talk, but I'll unblock you if you want to watch the dog like we discussed."

"Okay," he wrote back.

"This is your last chance to prove to me that we can be friends," I told him.

"Yes," he wrote. "I'll watch Nupa. And we can definitely be friends."

A few days later, I was ready and packed with a few hours left before check-in. Josh had arrived at my house and this time, I let him in. We hugged, a little awkwardly. I told him how much this meant to me and how glad I was we were able to rise above our issues and be good dog parents for Nupa. I had stocked the fridge with four days' worth of groceries so he could make himself feel at home. I figured this would be a nice break from sleeping on the floor of his studio. I walked him upstairs to the bedroom, showed him where her food and medications were, and set some money on the side table so he could take her to get her nails clipped. Her leash hung on the bed post for when he took her on walks.

"So as we discussed, you'll stay here at night and sleep with her?"

"Sure, babe. I promise."

I made a mental note—*if this goes well, and if he's up for it, he can come back in a few weeks when I have to go to Portland for Headbangers Con.*

He sat on the bed, lay back, and stretched out. Nupa jumped up next to him and nuzzled at his chest. I knew she missed him a lot. He looked at me and smiled.

"Take your clothes off."

"Excuse me?"

"Let's fuck before you go. It'll be hot."

"No! I have a plane to catch!"

He sat up. All hint of sweetness had evaporated. "Well, fuck you if you think I'm going to watch your dog."

Months and years of bile, anger, and outrage exploded out of me, splattering all over my bedroom thanks to Josh, who seemed to think it perfectly reasonable to expect sexual favors in return for dog-sitting services. I screamed at the top of my lungs that I had to catch a fucking plane and that if he didn't follow through on his commitment, I would never, ever speak to him again.

"Fine, fine. I'll watch the dog. Just quit yelling." He rolled his eyes, and I had never hated him more. But there was no time to find someone else to watch Nupa, and both my roomies were out of town. We would just have to make do. I peered under the couch, where Nupa was hiding. She hated it when we fought. "It's all right, girl. Mommy will be home soon. Uncle Shitface will take care of you."

✳✳✳

When I arrived in Louisiana, I messaged Josh.

"How's the dog? Everything okay over there?"

"Sorta. She had diarrhea and got kinda sick. You know how she reacts to your emotions."

"Did you clean it?"

"I'm cleaning it in stages because of my queasy stomach."

"So is my dog is sitting in her own shit right now?"

"I won't take this abuse, Bobbie."

Then he stopped responding to my messages. I tried calling him, but it rang and rang without going to voicemail. *The asshole had blocked me.* My daughter was sitting next to me as all this was going down. She gave me an "I told you so" look, pulled out her own phone, and sent him a series of well-composed, venomous messages.

Hello, asshole. My mother is crying right now. She's very worried about her dog. Would you please let us know what's going on?

I wished I had my daughter's composure, her ability to rise above and remain calm in emotional situations. She definitely didn't inherit that from me or her father. Josh wrote back to her that he refused to be verbally abused by me any longer, and assured her that Nupa was fine. He even sent a cute picture of the two of them together to underscore the point. Taylar showed me the photo and shrugged.

"Seems like she's okay, Mom."

I breathed a sigh of relief. "Thanks, Tay."

The next night, I took the red eye from Baton Rouge back to LA. I had popped a Xanax on the plane to help with my jitters (I hate flying) and arrived home just before sunrise. Groggy, I walked into my dark bedroom and called for Nupa. There she was, waiting for me on the bed. Bleary-eyed, I cradled her in my arms. My little girl. I was pleasantly surprised Josh wasn't there trying to get in my pants again. *Maybe he finally learned some manners,* I thought. Exhausted, I passed out on the bed with my dog, happy to be home.

***

I WOKE UP, STRETCHED out. Something didn't feel right. My face was all…itchy. I got out of bed and looked in the mirror. My right cheek was swollen and covered in hives. I looked back at the bed, where Nupa was trembling, a look of profound guilt and shame in her eyes. I pulled open the curtains, and when I let in the light of day, I saw the dried crusty shit stains on my pillow cases and all over the bed. Where I had been lying for the last eight hours. A whole world of shit.

In the corner of the room, the teeny tiny waste basket that I use for makeup was stuffed with shit-covered paper towels. The carpet was covered with oddly placed wee-wee pads, magazines, and little mounds of clothes. Underneath each, a patch of dried up dog shit. In the closet, dog shit under my shoes.

As I cleaned and scrubbed my room, my face covered with pink calamine lotion for the hives, I noticed the money I had left him to get her nails clipped was gone, but her nails were still long. Her leash hung beside the side of the bed, where I'd left it—he hadn't taken her for a walk once. This was so negligent, so irresponsible, so mean, it seemed out of character, even for him. That's when I realized this neglect was his payback for not sleeping with him. It was in this moment that I finally realized that I was truly done. We were no longer lovers, and after this, we could never, ever be friends.

He must have felt guilty because he tried to call me from Facebook. I blocked him there. Same on Instagram—I blocked him and had my daughter send him a message telling him to stop trying to contact me. This time, I wanted to truly shore things up on all fronts. His behavior with Nupa was the shit straw that broke the camel's back.

A few days later, I got an email from an address that wasn't in my contacts. "Oh, you want to fucking play mind games, huh? Well, get ready."

It was Josh. What he didn't realize, though, was that there was no game. This was it. Game over. I composed my reply.

"There's no need for you to threaten me. Nobody's playing games with you. I want nothing to do with you, ever again. Goodbye."

The next day, I registered Nupa as an emotional support dog, and when I went to Portland to do the autograph signing at Headbangers Con the following week, she came with me, sitting happily in my lap as I signed autographs with fans. We were fine on our own. We had no need for Josh or his dog-sitting services again.

BREADCRUMBING
AND OTHER SINS

I WAS FINALLY GETTING over my habit of zeroing in on the cute (young) bird with the broken wing. I wanted a happier, more secure future with a grown-ass man who would love Nupa as his own and never let me sleep in dog shit. A man who understood what it felt like to stand on a stage, deconstruct the anatomy of a joke, take life's tragedies and turn them into laughter.

A man like Jamie Kennedy.

I had been going through the online episodes of Jamie's podcast for days, fanning the flames of my crush. I watched him interview guests, talk about love and relationships. He wasn't frightened to go deep and ask the tricky questions, which I loved. He had this ability to really make people open up. If only he could open up *to me*. I could see us now, the comedic Beyoncé and Jay-Z, King and Queen of the Comedy Strip.

"Are you dating anybody?" I wrote him.

"Miss Brown! Why are you asking me that over text?" he responded. "That's something you ask in person."

"I'd be happy to," I said.

He never responded.

I didn't know what to think anymore. Drawn-out text conversations that went nowhere were really taking the wind out of my sails. Sharise told me to chill out. *Be easy-peasy. Don't message him so much.* She knows how to play this whole flirtation game. I don't. I don't do easy-peasy.

Maybe I need to be on his podcast, I thought. *Then he'll see how perfect we are for one another.* I sent a message saying that I should be on his podcast. His response was less than excited: "Don't be such a bulldog, Bobbie! Jesus!"

Bulldog? For daring to expect a direct answer to a direct question?

I pushed Jamie a few more times about the podcast, but the time between responses to my texts kept getting longer… and longer…until FLATLINE. He was ignoring me.

The Predict A Pen had been right after all. I just wasn't his type. Still, the not knowing was making me crazy. I just couldn't take it any longer. So I told him,

"I give up."

Immediately, a response.

"Don't give up."

✳✳✳

"He's breadcrumbing you," Sharise said after reading the thread of text messages between me and Jamie. "It's when they give you a little bit and they leave you hanging, and then they give you a little bit more and they leave you hanging some more. They leave you sitting on the bench because they might need you in case something better doesn't come along."

"How dare he engage in breadcrumbing at our age?" I fumed. "I just want to say, 'Look, are we doing this or not? How big is your dick? Do we have a future together or not? If not, then just tell me and I'll just move on.'"

Sharise shook her head and told me to calm down, that things aren't so black and white anymore. That no one is upfront and that they do have baggage and schedules and prior hurts that they are juggling alongside multiple dating profiles on various apps.

"Love's a game, Bobbie," she said. "You've got to study, learn the best strategies, think a move ahead, or you're always going to lose."

"Okay, Sharise," I said. "Show me how it's done."

Sharise sat me down in front of her computer and pulled up an article on self.com. "Knowledge is power," she said. "Read it and weep."

I scanned the article. "Benching" means "putting someone on the back burner, continuing to date them in a low effort way, because while you know you're not interested in them, you think they might have potential."

"Breadcrumbing," as the author defined it, is "flirtatious but noncommittal text messages to potential mates every now and then to keep them interested without exerting much effort."

Sharise was right. Jamie was totally breadcrumbing me!

I kept moving down the page. I knew what "catfishing" was, but what the fuck was "cushioning"?

"That's when you're flirting with a few different people while you're in a committed relationship," said Sharise. "So someone's there to cushion your fall if things go downhill."

"Deep Liking" is when you go far into someone's social media profile and like old posts.

"Is that bad?" I asked Sharise. "I do that all the time."

"Yes, Bobbie, it's bad. It makes you look psycho."

Oh.

Modern dating vernacular astounded me. "Dick Sand" is "the emotional quicksand that someone gets stuck in when infatuated with a guy." "Draping" is wallowing because you miss your ex. "Gatsbying" is posting on social media because you hope to get a single person's attention. *Guilty, as charged.*

A "Kittenfish" is someone who looks more attractive in photos than they do in real life, and "R-bombing" is reading someone's message and not responding to it. That, along with "phubbing" (when you pay more attention to your phone than to your date) is just plain rude. Freezing, tuning, penguin, shack pack, situationship, textlationship—truly, the new language of love lacks poetry.

I knew what "ghosting" meant, when someone just disappears, but I'd never heard of "haunting," which is when you ghost someone, but then pop back up on their social media. "Submarine-ing" is when you resurface without explanation after ghosting a person.

"Cuffing Season" is the time of year when perpetually single people get in a relationship during fall or winter because they don't want to be alone for Christmas.

"And then you break up just before Valentine's Day so you don't have to deal with buying flowers and chocolates for someone you don't really care about. Or you could break up just after, if you don't mind Valentine's with someone casual," said Sharise. "That's the uncuffing season."

Evil. Pure evil. All of it. All so calculated, none of it driven by of the pursuit of true romance or a great love story. Were we really just a society of convenience shoppers, using and trashing people like throwaway consumer objects? Did we really only view people as a temporary fulfillment of our need to have a date on Valentine's Day before putting them aside and getting back to the business of casual, noncommittal dating forever?

"Yes," said Sharise. "That's exactly what it's about. We'd better get used to it, Bobbie, because there's no going back."

Things were worse than I thought. Jamie was not only breadcrumbing me. He was R-bombing me, forcing me into a textlationship, and potentially benching me until the holiday season when he'd likely cuff me then ghost and potentially haunt and/or submarine me in the future. "Thank God I have you, Sharise," I said mournfully, cursing the misfortune of being a single, heterosexual, middle-aged woman in Los Angeles.

But Sharise told me not to worry. The new dating culture is only problematic if you focus on the negatives. But if you let go of jealousy, expectations, and old-school fairy-tale ideals, you can have a lot fun dating in the twenty-first century. It's a free-for-all, where you can meet a different interesting human every single night of the week if you choose. They may not be The One. They may not check your boxes. But maybe, if you're lucky, they'll take you on a ride. The rest is gravy.

TIGER DROPPINGS

I BOOKED A HEADLINER gig at Comedy Étouffée in Baton Rouge right before Christmas. I had called the venue myself and talked a good hustle, figuring it would be important to have a paying gig coincide with my visit home for the holidays. The next morning, Google, Social Mention, and Topwalker alerts started pouring into my inbox. I had set them up to notify me whenever anybody anywhere in the world mentioned my name online, including forums. A Social Mention alert led me to a local blog in Baton Rouge called TigerDroppings, named for Louisiana State University's football team, the Tigers. The headline was:

80s BR video vixen Bobbie Brown now doing stand-up

Someone going by the handle "the paradigm" posted that he had met me a few times fifteen years ago and that "at that time, she had been addicted to crystal meth." *Probably*, I thought. He said it was Tommy Lee who had introduced me to drugs, but that was wrong. I found meth all by myself with a little help from the modeling industry, which considers crystal meth a valuable slimming aid, up there with juice cleanses and Pilates.

She "was shacked up with some rich old dude in Malibu," the post continued." Wrong again. As already established, I am allergic to financially solvent men and have never dated anyone over the age of thirty-four.

"Theparadigm" capped off his reportage with this regrettable detail: "I could probably fill a small swimming pool with the amount of semen I rubbed out to her back in the day." Then, he posted a really horrible photo of me from about eight years ago, which he claimed is what I look like now. I cringed, cursing the Internet and wishing it had never been invented.

His buddies chimed in.

"Kingbob" described me as "an insufferable count," adding, "If she was hot, it'd be one thing, but she's all ate up with the fatness." I wished I were an Insufferable Count, being rude to my servants in some glorious castle in Europe somewhere—but probably he meant to call me a cunt. Being shamed for my body, my age, my past—it's water off a duck's back at this point. Hate is addictive, especially when it is spewed from the safety and comfort of your own computer without you ever having to look into the eyes of the person you're insulting. Cyberbullies tend to lack fulfillment in their IRL lives and the false sense of superiority they feel online can be addictive.

"btw-May have to rub one out to her tonight for old times' sake," "BuckyCheese" kindly added, as did

"HotCarl," who said, "I may have beat off to 'Cherry Pie' more than any other video in my youth. Billy Idol's "Rock the Cradle of Love" is probably up there too."

"Tgrbait08" said, "Used to go see her strip in Laffy back in the nineties." THIS IS FAKE NEWS. I've never stripped, and I don't appreciate being misrepresented in the media. Then they started saying mean shit about Taylar, how she was a cold bitch, and my patience ran out. I signed up for a TigerDroppings account with the name "bobbiejbrownbitches."

Time to set the record straight.

"First of all, that 'Now' pic you posted is seven years old," I wrote. "Do a current search if you want to be accurate. And ya, everyone knows I had a drug problem then, I wrote a bestselling book about it." I also said, "I have never stripped a day in my life. Do your homework."

The next day, I got a Social Mention alert leading me straight to another steaming pile of tiger turd.

"Bobbie Brown goes on a rant," it said, with "tgrbait08" insisting, again, that he saw me strip. "I saw you live and in person quite a few times stripping/dancing whatever you want to call it at a strip club in Lafayette back in the nineties. I even remember the perfume you wore. It was White Diamonds."

I was so mad. *White Diamonds*? The Elizabeth Taylor fragrance that smells like grandma's underwear?

I imagined myself coming back to Baton Rouge, being mocked by these guys, being shamed for my past, being judged for my body and the fact that I'm no longer twenty-one. Even for someone like me, a survivor of the most crassly misogynistic music scene ever, it's still challenging to navigate the hate and disrespect online, especially now that I'm older. I wondered if I should cancel the show—but I knew that would be a mistake. *You have to do this, Bobbie,* I told myself. You can't hide from the hate—you have to face it head on.

✳✳✳

People love to hate Bobbie Brown. They really do. My hate club extends across the continental United States, incorporates Alaska and several islands in Hawaii, and stretches into the Canadian territories and some parts of Mexico. It's like NAFTA, but meaner. Two haters have actively stalked me for years, *LaceyShore1* and *Sammi*[1]. The words they use suggest they're familiar with my reality show, *Ex-Wives of Rock*, and my first book, *Dirty Rocker Boys*. Every day, for years, they sent me little bundles of hate. *Every single day.* I wondered how they were able to juggle jobs, kids, and social lives while spending so much time dumping on my Facebook feed, spewing on my Instagram, and even sending hate mail to my personal email. I had to give it to *LaceyShore1* and *Sammi*—they were nothing if not committed.

I recently gave an interview where I mentioned that a storyline on *Ex Wives of Rock* that showed me buying my costar, Athena Lee (Tommy's sister), a pair of fake tits was, well, fake. Athena got the tits, but I didn't pay for them,

---

1   Names have been changed.

the show did. The interview came out and there she was, *LaceyShore1*, dumping a little basket of poop on my day.

"Can you believe it about Athena's tits? Bobbie Brown is such a fucking liar. She's always been a liar."

I very rarely block people who are not Josh, but *LaceyShore1*'s number was up. I hit "block." For good measure, I blocked *Sammi* too. Maybe they could get back to their jobs and families now and leave me the hell alone.

The next day, a message popped up on Instagram. It was *Sammi*, her tone unusually polite.

"Bobbie, I'm sorry. I know you're mad about me being a jerk to you. Now I know I was wrong. And please unblock *LaceyShore1*. She wants to apologize to you too." She explained that the *Sammi* on Facebook was no longer the real *Sammi*. "That's just a fake profile from people at my school. I go by *BillieChurch* now."

School? She was a high schooler?

"We are trying to change," said *Sammi*. "What we did is like Blue starting drama, because Blue was our favorite on the show, but we don't want to be like Blue anymore."

So they were fans of *Ex Wives*, and their favorite character was Blue! No wonder they were assholes! Blue Dixon, the ex-wife of Warrant's Jerry Dixon and my costar on the show, had always been unbearable to me. We'd endured several run-ins during the sixty-odd episodes, and one time I almost threw a drink in her face when she suggested that I had gotten thin by being on drugs again. She also accused me of using Jani's death as a ploy to sell books. Those dramas, unlike Athena's tits, were not invented by the producers. In Blue's opinion, I was nothing but a has-been who wrote a tell-all about her whoredom. "Which is rich," as I told her, "coming from a never-was." Clearly, as far as *Sammi* and her friends at school were concerned, the animosity made for great playground gossip. Knowing that these were teenagers helped me understand that they weren't mature enough to understand that Blue, Athena, Sharise, and I are real people with real feelings.

"I think you should change," I wrote to *Sammi*, trying to craft a gentle response for these young, impressionable minds. "Think about all the negativity you've caused and the time you've wasted doing it when you could be focusing on yourself, your friendships, your life, and your path, and finding what really makes you happy." I felt this was a "Come to Jesus" moment for them, a fork in the road. And I wanted to do whatever I could to help them become kind people, not cyberbullies.

"Only insecure and miserable people behave in ways that y'all have, and that's unfortunate," I typed. "Anyone with a heart would never want to be responsible for someone else's pain. Just think about that and remember, whatever you put out into the universe triples and eventually comes back to you. That's what they call 'karma.' Trust me, it really does work that way, I should know."

I never got hate mail from *LaceyShore1*, *Sammi*, or *BillieChurch* again. They were just kids, still figuring out that negative actions have negative consequences. Aren't we all?

ICE CREAM HAS A SOUL

Princess Poot

Once upon a time, long ago and far away
The whole kingdom gathered to celebrate a
special day
In honor of their princess, or so legends say.

She was lovely and lively and gentle and
Warm, full of compassion, and whimsy, and
Charm. Her eyes shone as bright as the full moon
At night, and she never did anyone any harm.

She was admired and adored by all, as she
Had been since she was small. Every lady and man
In the kingdom had come
To attend her debutante ball.

Now, in order for this tale to make sense,
You must first understand
That, years ago, a law had been instated in

The land, which declared the act of passing gas
To be
Universally banned. This sacred rule
Applied to each one of society's tiers. Never
Under any circumstance, could a fart be
Expelled from their rears.
Even in the king's palace this law was
Upheld. Not a poot could be heard, nor a toot
Ever smelled.

—Excerpt from *Princess Poot, A Children's Story*
by Taylar Jayne Lane

TAYLAR CALLED TO TELL me she'd written a book-length kids' poem called *Princess Poot* about a princess who farts. She said it was partially inspired by me, or at least, the persona she'd grown up with—the blonde, misunderstood starlet who tells fart jokes. Knowing that I wasn't the world's most stable parent, I take comfort in the knowledge that perhaps I've inspired her a little. And made her laugh. Like the time I saw mermaids on TV and called Taylar to verify whether mermaids are actually real, like Medusa. For some reason, I always thought there was an island of Medusas, somewhere in Europe, a short boat row from Mermaid Island. If there's one thing Taylar's always been able to rely on her mom for, it's entertainment.

For all we've been through, we're much closer than most mothers and daughters I know. Ours is a full-disclosure relationship; no topic is off limits, no subject too taboo to be discussed.

"You talk about *that* with your daughter?" people ask.

And the answer is *yes.* Anything and everything. When she started dating her first boyfriend at seventeen, she told me that they had tried anal sex. The next day I called her while she was at school and reminded her, "You know you don't have to do that, right?"

When I went on a date with Tom Green, Taylar was the first to hear about my experience with his iconic sole testicle. When Joey Fatone from *NSYNC tried to lure me into his bed by telling me that his dick was "the size of a tuna can," it was Taylar I called to help me understand what that meant. We were both very confused.

"Pretty much sounds like a mega chode, Mom," she said sagely.

Perhaps the reason Taylar and I get along so well is because she reminds me of her dad. Like Jani, she's an old soul. She's sensitive. She was the kind of kid who would cry if she dropped her ice cream. "It's just ice cream, I'll get you another," I'd say.

"No, Mom. It's not just ice cream. *It has a soul.*"

Taylar became disillusioned early on. She was more cynical than some kids and downright pessimistic at times. She knew the world could be evil, cruel, selfish, and unfair, and she learned a lot of difficult life lessons by watching me experience them. It made her tough—or, some might say, cold. At a young age, Taylar perfected her killer eyeroll. When she was a kid in Baton Rouge, soccer moms would come up to her in the street and compliment her on her white hair and big blue eyes.

One of my head shots

Me and my dog, Nupa

Me with my brother, Adam, his wife, Laura,
and their son, Ollie

My mom, Judy, me, and Taylar

Taylar and Daddy Tommy

Me and Gretchen Bonaduce

Me and Sharise meeting Leven Rambin, who plays Sharise in The Dirt

Me and my podcast cohost, Sharise Neil

Me and Caroline, my coauthor

Left: Jani Lane

Below: Josh, the millennial

Right: Tilky Jones

*My first stand-up appearance
at The Comedy Store*

*The girls after my comedy gig:
Stephanie Junco, Sharise Neil,
Donna D'Errico, and me*

Me and Donna at the Dojo

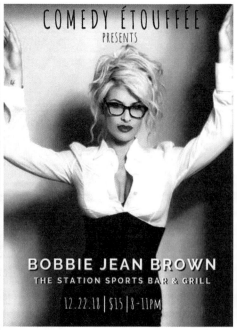

*The promo for my Christmas show in my
hometown of Baton Rouge, Louisianna*

*The dojo on my birthday with my comedy mentor Jimmy Shin
and his girlfriend, Erin Soto*

Performing at the Dojo

Flirty, forty-something, and funny as f**k…that's a saying, right?

"Oh, my gosh, your hair is beautiful. Where did you *get* that?"

"From my head, where do you think?" Taylar would say.

"By gosh, child, whose eyes do you have?"

"They're mine, duh."

She was five.

My mother would apologize for Taylar's apparent rudeness. "Sorry, she's from California," she'd say, and Taylar would fold her arms, annoyed.

She's just never suffered fools, not ever.

There's always been a palpable dynamic between us, kind of like close friends or maybe more like sisters, but also more than that. We make each other laugh and always have each other's back. There's always been an element of parent/kid role reversal in our relationship. Taylar has often described me as a childlike person with two sides: playful, affectionate, and imaginative on the one side, and irresponsible, temperamental, and chaotic on the other. Sometimes she felt like her mom needed to be taken care of more than her mom took care of her, so she tried over the years to be emotionally strong for both of us, at least as much as a child can be. We grew up together, and that made us closer somehow, although it wasn't always fair.

As an adult, Taylar suffers from anxiety—although, like a blonde Wednesday Addams, she'll never let it show. Instead, all her stress manifests as physical illness and if she doesn't process her feelings through her writing or work with animals, she becomes nauseated and gets terrible migraines. Of course, every time Taylar gets a headache, I feel crushed, guilt-ridden about my inability to be a "normal" mother. Although if you ask her, she'll say that she holds no bitterness toward me. For starters, she hates the idea of "normal." Her generosity and quiet dignity about the more difficult parts of her upbringing continue to astound me. Taylar's unconditional love brings me to my knees.

I wish I were an easier person. I really do. But things always seem to get so crazy in my life. So maybe it's no surprise that my daughter's adult life has been everything *but* crazy. Taylar's only had one boyfriend, and they've been together since she was seventeen. Financially, her ducks are in a row. She's been running Jani's estate since he passed away, and now, at the age of twenty-seven, she's a homeowner. She works at a dog boarding and grooming facility every day; I see her posting a pictures with a new dog every other hour, her eyes glowing with love for the animals.

I mean…she's pretty much a perfect human being. An upstanding member of society, an emo Steel Magnolia who has true love in her life and has somehow managed to avoid the worst traits of her addict mom and alcoholic dad. She's a miracle. I know Jani felt the same way.

✳✳✳

TAYLAR SPENT THE EARLY part of her life with Jani and I, until Jani strayed off the yellow brick road and set up camp at the bottom of a bottle of vodka. Much like my father, Jani was able to hide from his feelings for a while. I think Jani's addiction stemmed from his deep-rooted insecurity, his fear that his artistry as a musician would never be appreciated in the way he'd always dreamed. His manager and mentor, Tom Hulet, had managed the Beach Boys and Elvis Presley, and *that* was the kind of impact Jani wanted to make. It didn't matter that Warrant's five albums had sold more than ten million copies around the world; even "Cherry Pie," his biggest hit, our song, couldn't help Jani shake his underlying sense of frustration.

When we were living together, Jani was working on songs that he thought would cement his legacy as one of the greatest recording artists in rock 'n' roll. But by the time he felt ready to show the world what he was made of, the world had moved on. Warrant made it big in 1989, the year that the Strip started to lose steam. Kids who were disillusioned with hair metal's culture of ideocracy, misogyny, and crotch-grabbing excess were building a new scene around clubs like Jabberjaw, an all-ages coffee house and music venue on Pico and Crenshaw, where noise rock, lo-fi, and Riot Grrrl bands performed alongside rising indie stars like Kurt Cobain, Beck, Hole, and Elliott Smith. By 1989, the end of hair metal was already approaching. Grunge went mainstream with the release of Nirvana's *Nevermind* in 1991, the same year Jani and I married. Grunge swept Warrant and their glam metal peers out of the picture. Overnight, Jani and the rest of the peacocks became irrelevant buffoons in the eyes of the industry. Not mine, not Taylar's. But that didn't matter. If an artist loses faith in what they're doing, it doesn't matter what their family thinks.

Jani and I divorced in 1993 after just two years of marriage. He was cheating on me with the model girlfriend of Robbie Crane, the former bassist of RATT who had just joined Vince Neil's solo band. By this point, Jani's alcohol-related anger had become frightening. Shortly before his death he confessed to me that part of the reason he drank was because he'd been drugged and raped by a member of a famous heavy metal band and their manager when he was just starting out on the Strip. Stories of women being abused in the rock scene are all too common, but it is rare to hear about the male victims, perhaps because the stigma for them is so much greater. Jani was too ashamed to ever talk to anyone about it, and in the (understandable) absence of a #MeToo movement for male musicians, he suppressed his anger and used alcohol to tune out his feelings of shame.

Taylar went to live with my mother for a year while I tried to rebuild my life after the divorce. I'd always assumed once I got on my feet she'd come back to LA to live with me permanently. But fate had other plans.

When Tommy Lee, whom I had adored from afar since my teenage years, came galloping up in his red sports car, it felt like my knight in shining armor had finally arrived. He pursued me with a hunter's zeal, and when I finally agreed to sleep with him after three months of courtship, it felt like a dream. When Tommy and I got engaged, the dream felt like it was becoming reality. I truly believed everything was going to be okay, that it was a second chance for me and my daughter to be a happy family. Taylar even started calling him "Dad Tommy."

But yet again, behind the white-picket-fence fantasy lay two deeply flawed human beings, each battling their own egos and insecurities. Tommy was too possessive and tried to turn me into a perfect Southern Wife, cloistered in his beachfront home in Malibu. When Robert De Niro called the house, offering me an audition for the part Sharon Stone ended up playing in *Casino*, Tommy said no. He wanted me home with him. Staying home and cooking lasagnas for Tommy while isolated from my friends and family made me start to gain weight, which turned Tommy off. I asked an acquaintance from my modeling days if she had anything that could help me slim down fast. Soon I was in meth's grip, a paranoid tweaker, and my dreams of a life with Tommy quickly disintegrated. Taylar was there to witness it all.

One day, Taylar was living in a beautiful home on the beach with her mother and Dad Tommy; the next, Dad Tommy was holding her mommy up against a wall by her throat. It was all too similar to what I'd seen Bobby Gene do to my mom, and I knew I had to get out before things got much worse. I ended things with Tommy on account of the physical abuse, but even though I was the one who pulled the plug, it still destroyed me when he exchanged wedding vows with Pamela Anderson. She was blonder, made smarter choices, and was more famous than me. What little sense of self-worth I had evaporated, and all that was left for me was drugs.

I stayed with various friends, tried to get myself back on track, and jumped on and off the wagon. Taylar kept coming back and forth from Baton Rouge. She was maybe four years old. One time she wanted to go swimming at the pool where we were crashing, and I had been awake for a few days. I fell asleep, and when I woke up, Taylar was reaching into the water with her hand, with nobody supervising her. A vision flashed before me of her falling in and drowning while I slept. Had I not woken up at that very moment, who knows what could have happened? I beat myself up about it, vowed never to let her down again. I knew I couldn't keep that promise if I was using drugs—but I couldn't seem to stop.

I was in so much pain, I spent days in bed in the fetal position, crying and doing drugs. I tried antidepressants, but nothing worked. I could not fucking escape Tommy and Pammy, who were everywhere in the press. I had to feel the pain publicly and daily, and I couldn't function.

My mom said, "Get over it, he wasn't good for you," and I wished it were that easy.

Tommy and Pamela seemed to milk every photo opportunity they could. It was sickening, like they were forcing me to feel my failure every single day. The only way I could get out of my own head and escape the feelings of shame and humiliation was to get high. Finally, I understood what Jani and my father had gone through. Why they did the things they did. Why addiction is far more complicated than we're told, and how it's an expression of a lack of love for ourselves.

My weight dropped to ninety pounds when I was at my worst. I was partying, going out, and sleeping and eating only twice a week because I had to. I was falling asleep on modeling jobs and sending Taylar to Baton Rouge every few months because I couldn't cope, and then I was going to visit her and not being allowed to step foot in the house by my mom.

"I want to be with my daughter," I'd scream.

My mom would grit her teeth and say no. "You're staying at your dad's until you get your shit together." Before long, I made my mom Taylar's registered legal guardian.

Within a year of ending things with Tommy, I was a single mother with a drug problem and no home of my own. I wasn't able to take care of myself, much less my child. When Taylar was in LA she'd be on the couch or sharing a blow-up bed with me on the floor of a friend's house.

Taylar was in the eighth grade and was fourteen years old when she started living with my mom in Baton Rouge permanently. My two stepfathers, Mr. Earl and then Mr. Billy (aka William Williamson), also helped raise my daughter and loved her as if she was their own. When she misbehaved, my mother would say things to her like, "I'm going to send you back to live with your mom on couches if you don't get it together." It's sickening to think about. Even so, Taylar never, ever made me feel guilty about the choices I'd made.

There were many times over the years when I called my mom saying, "I just want to move home and be with my daughter."

But my mom wasn't prepared to disrupt Taylar's life unless I could prove I was ready to be a responsible adult.

"You can't come home unless you have fifty grand in the bank and are able to take care of her."

So, from a distance, I tried to teach Taylar to be a strong woman. To not make the same mistakes I did. To be confident, have a voice, and not let anybody put her under their thumb or ever treat her like she's second best—things that I allowed to happen to me.

One day, I finally went off drugs cold turkey. I slept for five days straight. I woke up clean, and all I could think about was how I wanted to make it up to Taylar. I wanted to be able to support myself and my kid. Then I'd have a little bit of downtime, and someone would offer me something, and I'd think to myself, "I'll be fine. I have it under control," which is the biggest lie an addict can tell themselves. Over and over again, I found myself back at square one. By the time I put drugs behind me, Taylar was already a woman.

Jani, for his part, spent the rest of his life punishing himself, his bandmates, and anyone who loved him. His demons clawed away at him until on August 11, 2011, he was found dead of acute alcohol poisoning at a Comfort Inn hotel room in Woodland Hills, California. He was forty-seven years old.

✳✳✳

ALL THOSE YEARS WATCHING her parents self-destruct took their toll on Taylar. As a teenager, she cut herself. Later, she started drinking—and heavily. For a while, we were terrified that she was following the same path taken by her father, whom she resembled so much in looks and in temperament now as well. But when Jani died, she was released. She stopped hurting herself. She started to talk about how she felt. She'd always written poems and stories, but for the very first time, she started to write poems about her father. Like this one:

Requiem for My Father
by Taylar Jayne Lane

I.

I wish I could have been
at the beach that day.
Not as your daughter,
but as a stranger
standing by.
It would have looked so beautiful
from far away,
without the film of tears
clouding my eyes.
But there is life
after death.
It takes not the shape
of angels, nor does it haunt
my unlit bedroom
like a ghost,
dressed in whatever clothes
you died in.
Instead, it enters
like a lightness

and it settles
in my bones.

II.
Your music lives inside me,
plays my veins with quick
fingers, like a
whorehouse piano man.
I float up
through your pale hair
like morning dew
ascends
to meet the rising sun.
And your sadness makes its home
in me, heavy
as an anchor,
sinking through me
like a stone.

III.
We spread between us
like a blanket
distance, at what cost?
So often we forget
to search for what
is not yet lost.
Before, if we had wanted
to, we might have spanned
the gap.
But now there lies

between us lands and rivers,
ever distant, which
no living soul can cross.
An army of the fatherless
stretches further than my eye
can see;
a flood
of mourning daughters
from the landscape carve
deep valleys with their tears.
With one eye, do you see beyond
the moss of death
to the vast deserts
of Truth?
With the other,
do you see
me?
Does it bring you
peace—that sweet
lightning—
when you behold,
in my verdant
fields, the weeds
and flowers of yourself?

IV.
I received no invitation
to your immolation,
but I will carry
in my heart the smoke

of your memory,
and the ashes
of what can never be,
but might have been.

V.

How sad it is to see
the dissolution of
a day.
How tragic that we fill
our hearts with names
that death can take
away.
The ocean pulled you
to it like the tide,
and left me lonely
on the shore.
I saw you, but only
for a moment,
as the great silence
fell once more.

A few years ago, after her father's death, the floodgates opened. Taylar and I finally talked about her childhood. About how I wasn't there. About my desire to make it in LA, and how that mission that had cost us both so much. If I could go back and change my lifelong dream to "make it," I would. You can't get back lost time with your child. That's why I am such an obsessive aunt to my brother's baby. I dote on the little lobster the way I wish I had doted on Taylar. *I missed my baby's childhood.*

When Father's Day comes around, Taylar and I don't really talk about it. Maybe I'll send her a message saying, "How are you today?" and she'll write back, "Fine, how are you?" Before my own father died, I was emotionally hard. I rarely cried. Now I cry at everything, all the time, every single day. I cry about my nephew, about my brother, about my mother, about everything. And I cry about my daughter, a lot. But all I have to do is hear her voice and the crying stops. At least for a while. All I have to do is eat ice cream and I'm reminded of Taylar. Cool, sweet, lovely, and full of soul. With a cherry on top. That's my girl.

THE DICKENING

IT WAS ANOTHER ONE-HUNDRED-DEGREE day in the East Valley, and I was rehearsing my set as Nupa watched me lazily from the couch. I had two fans on full blast, and as I stood in front of the full-length mirror with my bleach blonde hair blowing in the air, it occurred to me that I looked a lot like myself from the nineties. I could have been auditioning for a hair metal video, except now I had a few extra pounds and a dent in my head.

I assumed "comedy pose"—straight back, confident smile—and got to joking.

"People assume because I'm blonde and have big tits that I'm fucking stupid. I mean I *was* fucking stupid, but we broke up."

Nupa winked at me. Next to that joke I made a note—*okay*.

"I recently figured out that if I'm attracted to you, it's a good indication that you're a sociopath. It feels good to be self-aware. It's like halfway to healing, right?"

Meh. I crossed that one out and carried on.

"My ex and I had issues in the bedroom. Once during sex, he asked me to hurt him. So I said, 'You're never going to amount to anything, and I hate your new haircut.'"

I looked at Nupa. She was sound asleep.

"When I get lonely sometimes, I think about getting back together with him, but then I think I'd rather be reincarnated as an anal bead."

Not bad.

"I once told him to make love to me like we're in the movies, so he flips me over, comes all over my back, and screams his own name as loud as he can in my asshole. That's when I realized we don't watch the same movies."

Something about screaming into assholes has always appealed to me. A subconscious cry for help in the eternal void, aka: the Bobbie Brown Story. I made a note next to that joke—*good.*

My phone glowed on the bed behind me, and even though I was supposed to be practicing, I picked it up to check my messages. Maybe it was Jamie throwing me some of his crumbs. Alas, no. It was a dating app message from a guy with no profile photo. *Who the fuck goes on a dating app with no profile pic?* I thought. *I mean, if you're afraid of your own fucking face, so am I.*

That's kind of funny. I wrote the thought down.

Faceless Dude was asking me for nudes, so I responded with my stock answer: a photo of my favorite flesh-toned MAC lipstick.

He immediately wrote back, "Would you consider getting your breasts enlarged?" followed by a fairly lengthy description of how he liked to snort Viagra because of the way it knocks his dick out of his shorts. "I'll let you take the full six inches if you can handle it," he wrote. *This guy was so douchey it was almost entertaining.*

"Sure. May I also suggest an aggressive banana-eating contest with full eye contact?" I wrote, adding, "The winner gets to yell his name into my butthole."

My phone flashed again. This time it wasn't Faceless Dude. It was Jamie Kennedy.

"Hey, Bob. So yeah, I was thinking...do you wanna be a guest on my podcast? It'll only be an hour...unless we go down the rabbit hole of course."

This was no breadcrumb. This was a three-foot baguette. An invitation to sit face-to-face and confront our feelings in front of a couple hundred thousand of our closest friends.

A few days later, I found myself sitting in Jamie's studio, facing him, ready to go down whatever hole he wanted. He was behind his desk and talking into his mic, a copy of *Dirty Rocker Boys* on his desk. He was cute, and as always, his energy was a little guarded. I could not figure this guy out at all. I was dressed power-lunch casual, wanting to appear smart yet demure. By the end of the show, I wanted Jamie to understand that I was not just a demanding bulldog who texts too much and tells jokes about farting on men's balls.

I mean, that is me—but there's so much more.

"Ladies and gentleman, Bobbie Brown," Jamie said into the mic, adding, "not the singer—the other one."

My whole life, there have been too many Bobbie Browns. At castings, people often say, "Oh, my God, I'm wearing your lip liner!" to which I respond, "If I was a millionaire makeup mogul, do you really think I'd be auditioning for a Windex commercial?"

Then there's the R&B singer Bobbie Brown, whom I met in the nineties club scene. I'll never forget how his eyes lit up when I told him I was named after my dad. Months later, he conceived his own daughter with Whitney Houston (RIP) and named her Bobbi Kristina Brown (RIP), which added to the growing list of Bobbie Browns more famous than me. The most recent is Millie Bobbie Brown, who plays Eleven, the kid with the shaved head in *Stranger Things*. She's all over the Internet, all the time, and I get all of her Google alerts. It drives me nuts.

"So, are you nervous?" Jamie asked.

"Yeah. A little bit."

"Why are you nervous?"

"I don't know…I'm all ballsy and talky and whatever, and then when it comes down to it, I'm like…you know?"

Great answer, Bobbie.

"So, you're all talk no action?" he teased.

"Yeah. I mean. Totally, I'm normal."

"You're normal?" He raised an eyebrow.

"Yeah, totally. I'm normal." I nodded, cleared my throat. There was a tickle in it. I needed some gum. Water. A gun would be great.

"You're normal?"

"Yeah, I'm a normal person."

I pulled out my vape pen, took a drag.

"Is that weed?" asked Jamie.

"No."

"Regular smoking?"

"Yeah."

"What're you addicted to, nicotine?

"Yes."

"How long you been addicted?"

"Since I was in my twenties. But I quit smoking."

"Ever tried coke?"

A pause as we sized each other up. I wondered if this was a trap. Had he lured me on to his podcast to talk about how I had been a drug addict and focus on all the most uncomfortable parts of my life story? Was he going to Barbara Walters my ass?

"I'm a Gemini, you know," he blurted.

I was relieved. I preferred this direction. "A lot of people don't really get along with Geminis," I said.

"Why would you say that?" He seemed a little offended.

"Well, sensitive people can get confused by a Gemini because they have a tendency to say things that are mean," I said.

"We're *all* sensitive, Bobbie," he said.

I was starting to pick up on that.

Eventually we got to the nitty-gritty. The relationship stuff. It was harder than I thought, but I'd promised I would go down the rabbit hole with him, and now here we were.

"The reason my last relationship ended was because my ex spends the majority of his time with his dick in his hand, taking photos of it. Thousands. For anyone to do that many photo shoots of their own dick when they're not in porn is amazing to me."

Jamie laughed loud and hard. "She's funny! America, she's funny. Wait, so what...the guy had a photo shoot?"

"So many photo shoots."

"So much cock."

"So much cock."

"His cock."

"So much of his own cock."

"So, what's he working with? Nice cap on there? Was the angle like down there? Or was it like, pointed from across the room?"

"Um, up close. A lot of side shots."

Talking to Jamie about it was oddly therapeutic. I still had no idea if he was physically attracted to me; what was becoming clear, though, was that I was an object of mild fascination for him. A specimen, an animal at the zoo, an unidentified organism that he was peering at under his microscope, trying to understand.

"I figured something out about myself, Jamie, and it's horrifying," I said. "I have never dated a guy older than thirty-four."

"You like to ride that young pony. Can I say that?"

"Up to now, never older than thirty-four. What the fuck is that?

"Well, I mean, it's called honesty. You like what you like. And if you're a man at sixty in Hollywood, you're normal to never date over thirty-five. The fact that you're questioning it is awesome and fascinating. Why shouldn't you just date people who are thirty-five or younger?"

So many reasons, Jamie. But talking it through, I realized it wasn't just the sixteen-year age gap that had messed up my relationship with Josh. Cell phones, data, the fact that we live in the era of the dick pic. Or as Jamie put it, "The Dickening." The Dickening has taken a sledgehammer to love, made it nearly impossible to trust anyone with a cell phone and unlimited data. These days, for a man to cheat, he doesn't have to leave the house. Doesn't need to leave the bed he shares with you. As someone who has been paid a lot of money to share photos of her body with strangers, the entire concept of texting intimate photos of your most private parts to random people over Wi-Fi makes no sense. But for Josh, it was a daily source of endorphins. Sending pictures of his wiener into the Cloud was much more manageable than confronting the reality of a real relationship.

"Would you consider yourself Cougar Land?" Jamie asked.

"No! I'm not seeking out younger dudes. But guys my age don't like me. Is it because I'm not young or stupid enough?"

"You want to know why men your own age don't want to date you?"

"I told you I did."

"You might be a little bit of a tough cookie. You're a cool cookie. But I'm already getting a sense that you're a jelly cookie."

"What's that mean? A jealous person?"

"Yeah. And you might be a little bit of an HM cookie. High maintenance cookie. You might be a little bit of an 'I need attention' cookie. I'll tell you why, America. Because you were texting me and then you said something and then I didn't answer you back right away. And you said, 'You must be busy. I'll let you pack.' And I thought, 'That's interesting.'"

He's bringing up that text exchange from weeks ago?

"Because I didn't text you back in the timeframe in which you are normally used to," he said, "you chose to exit the conversation in a confrontational way."

"What?"

"You just *had* to say, 'I'll let you go.' As opposed to—"

"Just leaving it alone."

"Yes. Just letting it be."

Hm. Curiouser and curiouser. Maybe he was on to something. Even as a child, my mom would tell me, "Not another word!" So I'd walk up to her and crack my knuckles right in her face to let her know the argument was mine. But was this really the reason I was having trouble in relationships? My need to be in charge, to have the last word, to win the fight—perhaps it was a turn-on for younger guys, but not so much for older, more experienced gentlemen. The wheels of my brain started turning. So I'm supposed to be all Buddha now, *easy-peasy, lemon squeezy,* like Sharise says. But what if that isn't me?

"So do you want an LP or an FT?" he asked. "A life partner or a fun time, Bobbie?" I was grateful for the explanation.

"I think I've had enough fun times in my life."

"Have you? It seems like you've always kind of been relationshipped up."

"I've had relationships, but I've definitely had my party years where I was having fun and didn't want a relationship. And then I went completely celibate for five years."

Jamie's jaw dropped. Clearly, he hadn't gotten to the chapter in my first book where I describe how, after Tommy and I split up, I went on a year of revenge-fucking everyone in Hollywood followed by a good five years of nothing.

"Five years off the D Train?" he asked, fascinated. "And the P Train?"

"Yeah. Every train."

"Wow!"

"Not even the kiss train. Nothing. No BJs, nothing."

"No like, female friends hug you and it's like, 'Girl, let's have some tea. Ooh, let's watch a movie,' and then—"

"Eat pussy? No. I was literally skin starved, pretty much."

"Why would you do that?" Jamie asked. "Did you have that much sex that you needed to do that? It's not healthy. You gotta get hugged. You need kisses. Neck snuggles…"

I looked at him. I wanted him to snuggle my neck. I wanted him to snuggle my neck on the beach under a full moon. That would be nice.

He gave me a sympathetic smile. "You were seriously butt hurt, weren't you?"

"I was hurt, yeah. Yeah."

"This girl right here, she deserves love. She deserves intimacy."

What was he trying to say?

He picked up my book and gazed at the photo of me on the front in tiny denim shorts and bustier sucking on a lollipop.

"She was a little sex tart, so she came across a lot of plum pickers. The fact that you wore pants today, I was surprised."

"Gave the wrong impresh to a lot of men, is that what you're saying?

"Yeah."

I had given him the wrong impression. I had given everyone the wrong impression. Guys have always expected a certain girl when it comes to Bobbie Brown, the Cherry Pie Girl. They didn't know the real me.

"Welcome to being fucking sexy hot. It's a problem. You're a hot chick, right? Hot."

"Then, or now?"

"Both. Hot. You're hot AF. And back then, you were like the poster of hotness. That was your job. You were in the game. The Sunset Strip. When I was, like, fifteen and told my mom I wanted to be an actor, she was like, 'Okay, be careful of the Sunset Strip.' So you, as a woman who's hot, who's the epitome of it, deserve love and tenderness and huggies and kissies and nights in the park and holding hands. But you have to understand: A) what your position is, and B) what pool you're swimming in."

So, if you're looking for Prince Charming, stay away from the Sunset Strip, is what he's saying. But I'd already tried that, couldn't he see? I had changed. I'd stopped dating rock stars because it hurt too much. I'd dated a really normal guy, my handsome Josh who worked in construction and whom I'd loved with all my heart. I thought a regular guy would treat me well, worship me even. I was completely wrong. He wanted to break me down. I really, really didn't want to cry on Jamie's podcast. I held back the tears, but I think he could tell we were getting close to the bone.

"It's okay, Bobbie. I've stayed with girls who have literally stomped on my dick. And I've thought, 'I'm gonna let this this girl fuckin' shit all over me.' 'Cause you know what? 'Cause society says, 'This is what a relationship is, and this is what a good woman is.' Right? And then, after a while, you get away from it and you realize, 'Oh…' And that's the joke, Bobbie. Just because you're opinionated, that doesn't make you strong. It just could make you annoying. I like to be with people who are nice to me. You know what I mean?"

I did. I really knew exactly what he meant.

He looked at me and smiled. "People ask me sometimes why I do so much comedy. And I'm like, ''Cause comedy's always been there for me. Comedy is like the one woman in my life that's always been accepting of me.'"

I was starting to finally understand Jamie. The distance he maintained made sense now. Bobbie the Bulldog, who always had to have the last word and got pissy when she didn't get an immediate response, was probably a reminder of all the women who had pissed all over him before. Bobbie the Bulldog was a strong, opinionated bitch who would stomp on his dick, and/or annoy the hell out of him, given half a chance.

He had lost faith in love, as had I. And there we were, both experiencing the strange moment in life where you're not old, but you're not young any more either. Where you can't step back into the innocence that got you hurt in the first place, but you're not sure how to step forward. Could two such jaded people possibly get what they needed from one another in a relationship? I wasn't so sure any more. All we really had in common was our damage, and the strong, implacable sense that only comedy could fill the void.

Maybe that could be enough, for now.

BABY'S FIRST BOMB

I HAD LANDED ANOTHER show at the Comedy Store, and it was sold out. I was ignoring Jimmy's advice and still writing a new set every single time I performed. I was sticking to my theory that coming up with a brand-new routine every time was my "brand." It had worked for me so far, and tonight, my seventh show, I should have been feeling lucky.

As usual, I'd been up all night writing my set and hadn't taken the time to catch up on sleep during the day. I hadn't eaten, either, except for a few pieces of shrimp. Backstage, I downed two martinis, which I thought would settle my nerves. I stared at my notes, but the words floated around the page like vague acquaintances. I heard the host onstage introducing me with a declaration of my talents so flattering, so hyperbolic, I wished I had some kind of poison dart to shut her the fuck up. There was no way I could live up to that intro.

Applause indicated it was time for me to take the stage. I stepped up and took the mic, a full front row of people stared at me expectantly. All I could taste was fear and shrimp.

"So I'm driving fifty in a thirty-five, and this guy starts tailgating me. I remember thinking the lights on the top of his car look cool. Next thing you know, I've pulled over and am having the rudest interaction with this guy. He asks me, 'How high are you?' And I say, 'No, officer, it's hi, how are you?' He orders me to get out of my car. 'You're staggering,' he says, and I go, 'You're not a bad looking fucker yourself.'"

I really didn't want to be here tonight. I was a train about to hit the wall and everyone knew it. People shuffled in their seats. Suddenly it was too bright, too loud. Even my friends standing at the back looked afraid. We all knew what was about to happen. I was about to bomb.

"Uh, so I do yoga twice a week. By yoga, I mean I bend over to shave my legs, but even that's too much, and I've reached the age where my mind says, 'I can do that,' but my body says, 'try it and die, fat girl.' Even a loud fart throws my back out…"

Like a girl's first bleed or a boy noticing his balls are hanging lower than yesterday, bombing is an inevitable rite of passage all comedians must endure. But, as it happened to me, I couldn't help but feel sad that this had to happen in front of so many people. Innocent strangers who had paid twenty dollars in hopes of having their spirits lifted. Why make them suffer too? I needed this to be over, and not just for my own sake.

I talked faster and faster, rushing through my jokes like they were items on a shopping list. My poorly delivered gags blurred into one long bad joke that made no sense. The taste of shrimp and vodka martinis rose up my gullet as I raced faster and faster, tripping over my words.

"Hey, did you know that sometimes a lack of love from your parents leaves a hole in your heart only dicks can fill and, like, the hardest thing in the beginning of any new relationship has got to be learning how to fart quietly again?"

In my head, crowds in the Olympic stadium cheered as I crossed the finish line—*Bobbie Brown, fastest comedian on earth!* Then, I saw him. Jamie. He was there, watching me.

"Okay, thanks, sorry, bye!"

I raced for the side stage and barfed up those martinis and shrimp.

＊＊＊

"Tonight wasn't your night, was it, Bobbie?" Jimmy said afterward. I shook my head dejectedly.

"I should just quit, shouldn't I? I hate this feeling! I hate disappointing people, letting myself down, letting people down! *I'm always letting everyone down!*"

He listened patiently while I unloaded my shame and embarrassment. "I just thought I was breaking barriers by writing new shit all the time," I continued. "But it's exhausting, man! It's hard to do!"

He smiled at me, Yoda-like. "Exactly. You like to dive in, don't you, Bobbie? You have all this confidence, all this hubris, but sometimes it doesn't work for you. You got burnt."

Story of my life.

"Next time, you're going to get more rest the night before a show. You're going to be more prepared, and maybe not put so much pressure on yourself to always come up with something new. Dig deep. Perfect something, Bobbie. Then you'll never have to feel this way again."

I nodded, sniffling.

Jamie was waiting for me outside.

We sat down at a table. I felt close to him, not quite Bradley Cooper/Lady Gaga status, but like he was a mentor I had a crush on. Like I could confide in him and maybe we'd make out later.

"I don't know how I feel about this comedy thing anymore," I confessed. I rambled on, wallowing in my negativity and bruised ego. "It's too late for me, isn't it? I don't have what it takes."

"Let me ask you this, Bobbie—do you love comedy? Because if you don't, then you probably shouldn't pursue this life."

I nodded.

"But if you do, write yourself a set. Not just an okay set, a killer set."

He gave me an encouraging "pull yourself up by the boot straps" kind of smile. "Listen, Bobbie, how many people, after having the career that you've had, after everything you've been through—how many of those people get to be a stand-up comic to boot? This is the most difficult sport out there. Stand-up is going to open up so many doors for you, Bobbie, if you stick with it. If you can do stand-up, you can do anything."

If it hadn't been for Jamie, I probably would have walked away from it all that night. Instead, I left the Comedy Store determined to double down. And in a sense, I was relieved. I'd done it. I'd bombed. I'd hit rock bottom, and it was out of the way now.

The only way left was up. Right?

BLAST FROM THE PAST

Mötley Crüe Set 'The Dirt' Premiere Date
Seemingly unfilmable biopic will arrive
on Netflix next spring

—Rolling Stone.com

TOMMY LEE, VINCE NEIL, Mick Mars, and Nikki Sixx were all over the Internet, excited about their new movie, an adaptation of their band's bestselling biography, *The Dirt*. Vince Neil was so pumped, he used thirteen exclamation points in one Tweet.

"Wow!!! Just left Netflix offices. Just saw *The Dirt* movie!! Fuckin' awesome!! Can't wait for everyone to see it! Released March 22!! Yea!!!"

—Vince Neil, Twitter

Sharise was being featured in the film, which takes place during the years she and Vince were married. When she told me that Leven Rambin, the hot actress playing her, wanted to get in touch with me, I wasn't much in the mood to be helpful. The guys in the band were enjoying a second wave of fame thanks to the movie, but what about us, the ex-wives and fiancées? When was *our* story going to get told on Netflix or Hulu or Amazon? What we had to share was just as wild, just as fun, and just as watchable.

"So why does she want to talk to me?" I asked. "Is she researching Tommy Lee's sexual preferences as well as Vince's?"

"No, Bobbie," said Sharise. "She read your book, and she loved it. She wants to make a movie with you!"

Soon afterward, I found myself sitting in my living room with Leven, a refined blonde Texan in her late twenties with success is in her blood: her father being the owner of Houston's largest real estate firm and her grandfather being a former president of Texaco. She was making waves in Hollywood and looking for the perfect follow-up project to *The Dirt*.

Leven explained to me that as soon as she got the role of Sharise, someone had given her my book and suggested it could help with her research. It's not like Sharise was given much of a voice in the boys' book, but she was a huge part of mine.

"Reading *Dirty Rocker Boys* made me realize that someone really needs to make a movie or TV show about the *women* in that scene too, you know?" she said.

I raised my hands in a hallelujah. Finally, someone gets it.

"And of all the girls from that era, your story is the coolest," she continued. "It would be so incredible to play Bobbie Brown!"

She wasn't the first person to approach me about turning my story into a movie or TV show, but she seemed the best qualified and most sincere. Her energy was infectious, and immediately my chagrin about the Mötley movie lifted.

"So who was the person who told you to read my book?"

"My boyfriend," she said, smiling. "Actually, he's *in* the book. He's the guy in the boy band who you hung out with for a summer, remember?"

Tilky Jones. Southern boy. Oh, my God. How could I forget.

When I first met Tilky, he was in the boy band Take Five, which was formed by Lou Pearlman, whose other acts included the Backstreet Boys and *NSYNC. At the time, Tilky wasn't much older than eighteen, and I was already a mother in my thirties and heartbroken over Tommy Lee. That summer, we became friends. We even kissed, a little, although I knew better than to let it go much further than that. I'd always had fond memories of Tilky.

"Was he mad I, uh, mentioned him in the book?" I asked Leven.

"Oh, not at all," she said, looking at her phone flashing a notification. "In fact, he just texted. Can he come over? He says he'd love to see you."

Within an hour, Tilky walked in the door. The boy had turned into a man, and a beautiful one at that. He was an actor now, having appeared in *Pretty Little Liars, One Tree Hill, Single Ladies*, and a few films. I gave him a bear hug worth a couple decades, and we marveled at what a small world Hollywood really is.

"Bobbie, I'm so mad at you—why did you stop calling me?" he said, and I laughed. "No, seriously, Bobbie. What happened?"

He asked me how things were going and I told him about how I was starting a new career in comedy and working on a second book. I was also still trying to figure out my living situation—my roommates were moving out that week and I had no idea what I was going to do. We reminisced a little about the past.

"So why did you stop making music?" I asked. "You have the most incredible voice."

"I did the touring thing," he sighed, "and I hated it. Singing comes too easy to me; it's not something I learn from anymore. I like being able to put on a costume, Bobbie. I would rather play a part than reveal myself to the world."

Tilky sat next to Leven on the couch and picked up an old magazine with me on the cover. He stared at it, slowly shaking his head. "Man, oh man, oh man."

"What's wrong?" I asked.

"Nothing, Bobbie. Except, look at this. Can you believe this?" He held up the magazine. "You, Bobbie. Eternal fucking hotness, right there."

I knew Tilky was just being flirty, having a little joke. I really hoped Leven saw it that way too.

"Well, thanks for lifting a tired old lady's spirits!" I said, snatching the magazine from his hands.

Tilky piped up. "Don't put yourself down, Bobbie. You're the sexiest woman in Hollywood, hands down. Isn't she, honey?"

Leven smiled. "She's gorgeous. An absolute legend."

After they left, I sat on the couch and began composing a text to Leven. It basically said how lovely it was to meet her and how I couldn't wait to work with her. Then I got a text message, from Tilky.

"I miss you so much."

Wait. Was he *flirting* flirting? I couldn't tell. I'd assumed he was just being extra friendly, but maybe there was more to it. It was so hard to tell, but either way, I've always had a strict girls-first policy. My code of conduct dictated that I should immediately tell Leven that Tilky was being flirty with me. Or something. So I did what I thought was right. I forwarded the message to her, with a note:

"I don't want there to be any weirdness or secrets between us," I wrote her. "But you should know, Tilky just sent me this."

Within minutes I got a call—from Tilky.

"Why the hell would you do that, Bobbie?"

"Well, I don't think it's cool to flirt with me if you have a girlfriend," I said. "I just thought that it should be addressed."

He laughed. "Jesus, Bobbie, I'm just being friendly. Why do you have to be such a drama queen? And by the way, Leven says it's very nice how respectful you're being, even though it kind of wasn't necessary."

"So you weren't flirting with me?"

"I don't think so? Either way, I kind of flirt with everyone, Bobbie. I flirt with eighty-five-year-old diner waitresses."

I could hear Leven in the background shouting, "It's true, he does!"

"Oh."

Perhaps it's my PTSD from being on the Strip in the eighties and nineties that's made me so militantly protective of women. I've seen what happens to us out there, and it ain't always pretty. For so long, there was zero protection for us in this town, at least until the #MeToo and Time's Up movements came around. I've always tried to be a one-woman "Time's Up" movement, a mother hen calling out bad behavior in public and telling girlfriends the truth about their men, even if it sometimes cost me a friendship. But for some, ignorance is bliss, and I've been branded a shit-stirrer. And even worse is when I get it wrong.

And so, by trying to do the right thing, I could have totally pissed off that nice Texan actress who wanted to help me and all the girls I came of age with while alienating my long-lost friend to boot. Luckily, neither of them took it to heart, and Leven continued to champion the idea of a *Dirty Rocker Boys* movie around town. Turned out, the world wasn't quite ready for the girls to have their moment. The powers that be were unsure about making a film that dished on every leading man in Hollywood, especially if it meant dealing with lawyers representing Leo DiCaprio, Tommy Lee, and Kevin Costner. It all felt very unjust. Still does, if I'm honest.

THE BABE STATION

In response to the messages sent to her by readers of her 2013 Kindle bestselling memoir Dirty Rocker Boys, *Bobbie Brown returns with a second helping of cherry pie, serving up raucous, candid advice on love, sex, and dating, with a generous side of Southern sass...*

—Promotional material for *Cherry On Top*

CAROLINE RYDER, MY WRITING partner on *Dirty Rocker Boys*, arrived back in LA from London, ready to get to work on the book you're reading now. She showed up at my house—blonde, artsy, and diminutive—wearing a denim jacket with an Andy Warhol pin on her lapel. We come from different places, yet we share a fair amount in common. We are each eldest daughters who left home to pursue the Hollywood dream. We are die-hard romantics. We have racked up countless parking tickets. We have Chihuahuas. We love shrimp, *RuPaul's Drag Race,* and astrology. And both of our moms are named Judy. We've always had great creative chemistry.

I showed her in and asked her how she was doing. She was worried about her brother. "He wrote a novel about an Incel who jumps off a building. He says it contains autobiographical elements."

"What is an Incel?" I said.

"You don't wanna know, Bobbie" she said, sighing. "It's these young guys who have trouble finding girlfriends and are angry about it, so they talk shit about women on the Internet, which makes them feel like they have a sense of community. But sometimes they murder people and/or themselves."

"Oh," I said. "I'm pretty sure those guys follow me on Instagram."

She pulled out her voice recorder and hit "record."

"So what's been going on, Bobbie?"

Before I had a chance to answer, an attractive, sleepy man wearing nothing but a Gucci silk robe wandered into the room.

"Nice robe," said Caroline, looking at me, confused.

"Yeah, it's Bobbie's," said the man, adding, "I feel terrible, let's have a drink."

It was Tilky.

So let me explain. After our unfortunate text interaction, Tilky and I had resolved our differences, but had fallen out of contact again. Then, all of sudden, I started thinking about him, and I wasn't sure why. *Something's going on,* I thought, so I sent him a message.

"Your name keeps popping into my head, so I'm just sending you a text to say 'hi.'"

He responded immediately. "Leven and I broke up. I'm not doing good."

I told him I was sorry. If he needed to talk about things, I'd be happy to.

He showed up at my house, looking like he hadn't slept in a year. I showed him in and sat him down.

"Can I tell you something? I hate myself," he said.

"Believe me, I know exactly how that feels."

He asked for a cocktail to settle his nerves.

I made him a vodka tonic and asked him to tell me exactly what happened.

He told me he had just moved into a new house with Leven, but then she told him they needed some time apart. He was very much in love with her, so this all came as a shock. She promised him that after the break, she'd be willing to discuss him moving back in and picking up where they left off. Tilky left town to film a movie in Florida, then, when he returned, she told him it was over for good.

Since then, he'd been on a mad bender, going from this girl's house to that girl's house, this party to the next. All of his belongings were stashed with a friend, all hope and sense of home had blurred in a cloud of heartbreak and liquor. Lord, if I didn't know exactly what that felt like, living moment to moment and only finding comfort in the promise of tonight's escape. I told him that he'd feel better soon. That breakups are the hardest thing on earth, but they usually lead you to a better place.

I handed him some Kleenex, put a shrimp and artichoke dish on the stove, and just let him get it all out of his system.

"I'm looking to be with somebody. I'm a Southern guy, I want a family. Bobbie, I just want to stop. I want to rest."

I told him all that would come for him in due course.

He nodded. It was getting late. "Bobbie, can I just lie down for a while? I feel horrible."

"Sure. Do you need some water or something?"

"No. I just need to lie down."

I took him up to my bedroom. He took off his shirt and lay down on the bed.

"Can you come here for a second?" he said, tapping the edge of the bed.

I hesitated, unsure of what he was doing. I sat next to him, warily.

"Bobbie," he said, taking my hand. "You were so beautiful back then."

"Great. Thanks."

"And you're still beautiful. In my eyes, you haven't aged a second."

"Thank you. That's very sweet."

"I was a little intimidated, but the coolest memories that I have from being a teenager were from that summer with you. I've thought about you for years. You know, I've always loved you…"

I pulled back my hand. This was too much. "Shut up, man. You think that you can just come over here and fuck me to make yourself feel better? Huh?"

He apologized, profusely. "No, Bobbie, it's not about that. I'm telling you the truth. I really do love you. It's not about sex."

"Yeah, right. How can you tell the truth when you've been drinking? You've been drinking a lot, haven't you?"

My heart was pounding. Another bird with a broken wing—too young, too handsome. Was he just being flirty, like he said he always was with women? Does he tell eighty-five-year-old diner waitresses they're beautiful too? Danger bells clanged in my ears, and I stood up.

"Listen, panty dropper…I think you better stop this. A girl can get really attached to that kind of romantic, sweet talk, and it's not fair. You don't know what I've been through."

Tilky nodded. "Bobbie, can I stay for a few days?"

I had no idea what to do. Whether to hold his hand or kick him to the curb. With all the pain I'd been through, and all the determination I needed to restart my life, it was really easy for me to see Tilky as a threat. But he was polite. Unlike Josh, he wasn't trying to pressure me into anything. Most of all, I got the sense that he needed a friend. Someone he could trust. The downside of being a nice person in Hollywood is that people tend to wind up on your doorstep when they're down. People like me, Gretchen, and Sharise—the nice girls, the mama bears— we really are few and fucking far between. And sometimes it's hard to figure out when these cries for help are real, and when we are being taken advantage of.

Tilky is an actor, but all alcoholics know how to play a role. And I wasn't sure how much of what he was saying to me was sincere and how much was a way to reel me in emotionally, turn me into a soft place to land.

A babe station.

The guys who babe-station hop from girl's house to girl's house say all the right things. They lure you in and get the attention they need from everyone, all the time. They can cry on demand because they cry for themselves and their lives, which are slowly slipping out of control. They stare deep into your eyes without flinching. They ooze charisma and charm. They are entitled and spoiled, shrouding themselves with negative thoughts. Nonetheless, I dote on them, take care of them, help them with anything they need, include them in every detail of my life even though their words and actions are rarely in line with one another.

Unless they're obvious about it, most times I will not be able to tell if they're using drugs or alcohol because while I may be used to addicts, I still don't understand the disease. Instead, I'll find myself in another disappointing relationship or friendship in which my expectations are unreasonably high and then feel unappreciated as I continue to do way too much, all the while asking myself, *Why am I doing this? I am a grown ass adult. I'm not stupid. I'm not in love.* And then I realize I do this because I don't want them to die.

As Tilky lay sleeping on my bed, I worried that I was overthinking things. But I had to stay vigilant. I had only just gotten my life back on track after Josh. I wasn't ready to embark on another all-consuming journey, if that's what this was. I couldn't tell. Men are my kryptonite, this much I know, but it is my destiny to love and help, to be of service the way my mother was, and the way my father eventually was too.

I tried to imagine what my dad would say to me in this situation. He would tell me not to beat myself up for having a heart. That my heart was the thing he was proudest of. I thought about Jani, how right before died he reached out and asked if he could come and live with me.

I'd said no.

I looked at Tilky and knew I couldn't say "no" anymore. I wanted him to know how much someone cared. I wanted him to know how special, how beautiful, how talented he was, and that there was no need for him to feel alone or without family because *he mattered*. I decided to try and show him all of those things and make him understand that there is no need to disappear. Even though the thought scared me to death.

As he slept, I went in the hallway, called Taylar, and told her what was going on.

"Mom, this is probably a horrible idea. You know that, right?"

"Are you mad at me?"

"Mad? About what?"

"That I always seem to find myself in the same situations."

"Mom, at a certain point I realized there's no point in getting mad," she said. "You're just going to do what you do. This is just who you are. Maybe it's an abandonment thing, like you're afraid of ending up alone and not married or whatever. Or maybe you just really do believe that these guys are good people deep down. I hope you're right."

I hoped so too.

THE EMPEROR'S NEW CLOTHES

IN NOVEMBER 2018, THE City of Angels found itself ringed by infernos. It was the deadliest and most destructive wildfire season ever recorded in California. Some said the fires were headed in my direction. Even so, the show must go on.

Jimmy called to say he was putting together a show at the Dojo that Jamie Kennedy was headlining, and he wanted to know if I would be interested in performing too. I hadn't been in touch with Jamie much recently, nor Jimmy. My attention had shifted since Tilky showed up at my door. See, that's what happens when a man comes into my life: tunnel vision.

Tilky had stayed a couple of nights and said that being at my place and away from the party scene had made him feel better. My roommates had moved out and the obvious conclusion was, *Why doesn't he just move in?* He wanted to. He had money saved. He was tidy and trustworthy.

He was a friend. It seemed to make sense, but still I felt like a moth, flirting with the flame that might kill it.

"Bobbie?" Jimmy said on the end of the line, impatient for an answer.

Oh, yeah. "Go ahead and put me on the show billing. It'll be nice to see Jamie."

I sent Jamie a message, letting him know I'd be sharing the stage with him again. Feeling guilty for going a little cold on him, I added that I had a hook-up for a great men's clothing wholesaler that supplied me with items for my own online clothing store.

"Would you like some cool new designer sweaters?" I asked him, sending a link to the wholesaler's stuff.

He said he liked three sweaters.

"Great, I'm on it!" I said, guilt instantly relieved to be doing a nice thing for him. I hit up the wholesaler and told them I was ordering clothes for a famous comedian. Maybe they'd be interested in sponsoring him, if he wore their stuff on social media? They said they were fans and would love to. I was so proud of myself. I love helping people out, even if it is for selfish reasons. All was well with the world.

A few hours later Jamie's assistant emailed me with instructions to have the clothes sent directly to his house. This couldn't happen; the pieces would have to come to me first, and then I would send them on to him. His assistant did not seem to understand, so I explained again.

"They don't sell to just anybody. You have to have a wholesale license and all kinds of shit. Anyway, we don't need to get into a confusing saga—when the stuff arrives, I'll just drop it in the mail to you. Cool?"

The clothing arrived, I opened the package, and it all looked great, so I sent Jamie a message letting him know his new threads were in. Instead of the profuse thanks I was expecting, I received a curt "Why wasn't the clothing sent to my home?" I told him I had already explained to his assistant that everything was coming to my address because this is where my online store is located.

"What store?"

Why is he asking me all these annoying questions? I thought. I explained that I have had an online business for years, selling vintage and designer clothing that I store in my garage.

"So where is this 'store' located, Bobbie—your bedroom?"

"No…" I said, annoyed to be wasting time on this. Nonetheless, I sent him a link to my website. "Look, see? What fucking difference does it make anyway? And by the way, you're welcome."

"Was I supposed to say thank you?" was his cold, rude response.

Yes, you asshole. Yes, you were!

"You do realize I got you a really great deal, and now, by the way, they'd like to sponsor you?" I wrote, my blood beginning to boil. "That was all because of *me.* But you're being a jerk and I don't know why I'm even trying to be sweet to you. It won't happen again."

Perhaps he was just trying to push my buttons. Perhaps I was pushing his. But what happened next was so ridiculous, so pointless, I'm still sort of confused by it. All I knew was that I wanted the last word, and I was going to have it.

"YOU CAN TAKE YOUR SHIT ATTITUDE AND SHOVE IT UP YOUR ASS, AND THEN SHIT ON SOMEBODY WHO DESERVES IT, BECAUSE I CERTAINLY DON'T."

I felt nauseated watching the little bubbles bob up and down on my screen as he composed his reply.

"Bobbie. You sold me clothes, I bought them. You know how many people offer me clothes? Lots. Relax. I have lots of sponsors. And you have mad entitlement issues. Just tell me the address to your 'store' and my assistant can come pick up the clothes, but I suggest understanding your personal issues before lashing out at people."

The text box may have been blue, but by this point, I was seeing red. I didn't understand where he got off saying I had personal issues just because I expected a "thank you." This felt like a power play, and I knew I was falling for it hook, line, and sinker. He wanted me to lose my temper, he wanted me to make a fool of myself. But I had to set him straight.

"JUST BECAUSE I'M NICE, IT DOESN'T MEAN I'M BENEATH YOU, OR DON'T DESERVE APPRECIATION FOR MY EFFORTS I BESTOW UPON YOU, MY MISTAKE. OH, AND THAT'S SOOO GREAT THAT YOU HAVE SOOO MANY SPONSORS. JUST BECAUSE YOU GOT MAD SPONSORSHIP DOESN'T MEAN THAT YOU SHOULD BE UNAPPRECIATIVE."

Really, I ought to have left it there. That would have been the smart thing to do. But I've never been good at knowing when to stop.

"OH, AND IF YOU'VE GOT SO MANY MAD SPONSORS THEN THEY'RE SHITTY BECAUSE YOUR STYLE AIN'T THAT FLY. YOU SHOULD BE THANKFUL. GEEZ, GET OVER YOUR FUCKING SELF AND STOP ACTING LIKE A PRIMA DONNA. GET A CLUE WITH YOUR RUDE ASS AND RELAX, YOU MOODY FUCK."

I hit "send" and threw my phone on the bed, seething.

And then a few seconds later I remembered I was supposed to be sharing a stage with him that night at the Dojo. *Shit.*

***

THAT EVENING I WAS at the venue having an early dinner with Jimmy. Tucked beneath the table, by my feet, was the bag containing Jamie's damn clothes. I figured I would give them to him and we would make our peace somehow. Obviously, things had gotten way too heated, as they sometimes do via text.

"Things get lost in translation, don't they?" I said to Jimmy, through a mouthful of noodles.

"Sometimes," he said, shaking his head as I explained that afternoon's unfortunate events.

I saw Jamie walk into the venue. He saw me too and walked right back out again.

"That was weird," I said to Jimmy, who stood up, went out to the hallway, and came back a few minutes later.

"He wants to talk to you. He's very upset, Bobbie."

This irritated me. Why do I have to get up and leave my noodles for this shit?

"I'm eating, I'll go talk to him when I'm done," I said, grumpily.

Two minutes later, Jimmy came back. "Bobbie, we have a situation. He's refusing to go onstage until you go out there and talk to him."

I marched into the hallway, holding the bag of clothes. Jamie was pacing in the back corner by the men's bathroom. When he saw me, he held his phone up in the air, as though it was evidence of some crime.

"I'm not performing tonight because YOU ruined my day. YOU brought negativity to my day when you attacked me for NO reason, NO reason at all. You're crazy, Bobbie. You're insecure!"

I started laughing.

"This is serious!" he screamed at me.

"Whoa, slow down, dude," I said, stunned by how angry he was. "You can't just stand there waving your phone around acting like you weren't trying to press my buttons with the things you were saying. You didn't even say thank you!"

"I wasn't trying to push your buttons. You're just insecure and that's your biggest problem, Bobbie."

I flung down the bag of clothes. "Look, asshole! Bottom line is, you didn't think that I deserved thanks for my efforts, and I don't deal with unappreciative people, okay? That's not my fucking job. I went out of my way to be nice to you, but that's okay, you do you. Peace out, whatever."

I turned to walk away, and he said, "Look at these messages! You attacked me!"

The MC was calling him to get on stage, and here we were, fighting in the hallway. I turned to him and snarled. "Just get up on stage and do your fucking job."

His eyes darkened. "You don't talk to me like that."

"Why not? Who are you anyway? You rude fuck."

He started yelling. "I didn't do anything wrong! I DIDN'T DO ANYTHING WRONG!"

"You didn't do anything right, either."

I went to the bathroom for a second and tried to compose myself. When I came out, I heard Jamie, on stage, telling the whole audience what had happened—from his perspective, of course.

"Crazy, right?" he said, as the audience laughed. "She asked me to buy her clothes, so I buy her fucking clothes, then she's like, 'You ASSHOLE!'"

He had turned our private fight into a comedy bit. I couldn't believe it.

I had to see this with my own eyes or else I wouldn't believe it was happening.

"Oh, there she is, right now," Jamie announced, all heads turning to face me as I walked into the room. "Come on in, Bobbie Brown."

I looked at him and shook my head. "Are you crazy?" I hissed. "Are you OUT OF YOUR FUCKING MIND?"

The room was dead silent in anticipation.

"You think *I'm* the crazy one?" he said.

Disgusted, I walked into the hallway, and screamed, "FUCK YEAH, YOU ARE," hearing the whole room erupt in laughter behind me. It might have been my greatest moment as a stand-up comic, and I wasn't even in the room.

"Go get her!" I heard Jamie yell to the security guards. "You guys want to see a live fight on stage right now? Go get her!" The security guy came out into the hallway, looking for me, but I was too fast. I marched outside, uninterested in being publicly derided by a man I thought was my friend. *He's got the mic, and I'm going to look like an asshole if I get on that stage. I'll never get the chance to explain myself.* I sucked hard on my vape pen, shaking, and sent Jimmy a message, my hands trembling.

"I'm so sorry," I said, "I don't know what happened."

"Don't worry, Bobbie. Are you okay?"

I wasn't okay. I was too new, too fresh on the comedy scene to be having mad beef with established names. I still didn't understand what had just happened. Why had Jamie acted like that? Rich and famous Jamie, with his 175k followers, his assistant, and personal podcast studio in his fancy fucking home. Why would he act like that?

It was my mouth again. My mouth had gotten me on stage, and it might well get me kicked off it, too.

Tilky, Caroline, and I sat around a steaming bowl of boiled shrimp and artichoke the next morning, deconstructing the strange events that had transpired at the Dojo the previous evening, which had apparently sent shock waves through our little comedy community.

"From a man's perspective, what do you think that behavior was all about?" Caroline asked Tilky.

"Well, clearly, he's a control freak," said Tilky, frowning at the shrimp, the odors of which were not pairing well with his hangover.

"Bobbie, did you feel you were close to him?" asked Caroline.

"Not really," I said, standing by the microwave, melting the butter into which I would soon mix lemon juice. "I mean, not physically. But I'm his friend. I got him a clothing sponsorship for crying out loud. Is nothing sacred?"

Tilky came up with a solution. "I'll beat his fucking ass." Then he thought about it. "Actually, maybe he did you a favor. Because everyone in that room will be like, whoa, *Bobbie Brown.*"

"No, I think that's an optimistic view of events," said Caroline. "But I do think this is probably the first time in a long while that someone's treated him like a normal human being, Bobbie. You called him on his attitude and now he totally hates you."

Caroline saw this as another great story for us to write about, but that's my problem. My life was full of great stories that were funny to the outside world but awkward as hell for me. I mean, Jamie was the closest thing to a real comedy boyfriend I had. I was just benching him for a bit while Tilky took up my attention. But I still wanted him around. I didn't want him to hate me. He was supposed to give me neck snuggles one day, and then we'd live funnily ever after.

Tilky looked at Caroline. "Who are you, by the way?"

"She's my cowriter and friend, Caroline," I said. "We've been working together for a while—six, seven years?"

He cocked his head to one side, sizing her up. "So, you just came all the way from Europe and…"

"Yes, and now I live here," Caroline said, looking at him. They observed each other for a moment, silently.

"Have you ever considered writing a Christmas movie, Caroline?" Tilky asked.

"No."

"I have this idea called *Santa Cruz Christmas*. A Christmas surf movie."

"You mean like surfboards and Santa Clause but there's vampires, like *Lost Boys* meets *Elf*?" she asked.

"I don't know about the vampire part," said Tilky.

"You're wrong," Caroline said. "Santa is definitely a surfing vampire."

"You're going too far with this, Caroline…and, by the way, did you know you're beautiful?"

Caroline, caught off-guard, blushed a little. "Oh, me?"

"Not just because of this"—he made a sweeping motion that indicated her face—"but because of this," he said, tapping his temple. Tilky the panty dropper had struck again. He just couldn't help himself.

Caroline cleared her throat. "Anyway…so, uh, what happened next, Bobbie, with Jamie?"

I sighed, setting the melted butter on the table. "What happened next is that I haven't heard from him. He didn't call to say sorry, and even if he had I wouldn't know because I blocked him on all platforms."

Caroline shook her head, surprised. "You *blocked* him? Why?"

Truth is, even though Jamie overstepped the mark—I mean, he ripped me onstage and *still* took the fucking clothes home—I blocked him because I was afraid of what else he might say to me, and that it might ring true on some level. I didn't trust myself to stay calm if that happened. Bulldog Bobbie is real, something Jamie had picked up on from the first moment he met me. Blocking him was not just a way to avoid him, but to avoid inflaming the part of my soul that still feels wounded and cornered by life. The part that snarls and snaps when it gets hurt. The part that has to have the last word, even when it would be smarter to just walk away.

Caroline frowned. "He's quite well-known, isn't he? Will this affect your comedy career?"

"I don't know, maybe?" I replied dejectedly. I really hoped not.

"It won't, Bobbie" said Tilky, supportively. "It's going to blow over, then one day you'll cross paths and it'll be cool."

I smiled, grateful for his optimism. Grateful for him.

SAD CLOWNS VERSUS
THE WORLD

I READ A BIOGRAPHY of Marilyn Monroe in which the author described walking down the street with her, how she purposely drooped her shoulders and stared at the ground so that nobody would recognize her. Then, after a few blocks she said, "Watch this." She pushed her shoulders back, pouted her lips, and unleashed her strut. Within minutes, she was mobbed. "Marilyn" was a character Norma Jean played, and she could turn it on and off at will. I wished I could do the same with "Cherry Pie Girl."

For years, I felt like when people met me, they expected the character Jani and I had created in that video. The freewheeling sexpot with dozens of lovers, playful and coy; she'll make your fantasies come true, like some kind of walking, talking blow-up doll in a red bustier and denim shorts. But that's not really me. (Though, truth be told, cherry is actually my favorite pie.)

Over the years, this has put me in a lot of awkward situations. I'd go on dates with guys, and they'd act disappointed when they realized I wasn't going to let them cover me in whipped cream so they could lick it off. Mostly I would make silly jokes and offer them a sandwich—things that I think are nice.

But guys don't always want nice. They want the hotchacha, the fantasy. They're not interested in my sense of humor, my conflicted feelings toward fame, the way I teeter-totter between supreme confidence and crippling insecurity. That's the stuff that doesn't make sense to them. The stuff I usually keep inside.

Only a handful of people "get" the real me, and one of them is Tilky. As soon as he moved in, with his little suitcase and the first month's rent check in hand, we were official—two sad clowns versus the world. He fell quickly in line with my off-color banter and we'd spend hours going back and forth, playing quick-fire mental ping-pong. We'd wrestle for a while and round out the day with a facial—or maybe we'd color our eyelashes. I never thought I'd be able to feel any kind of closeness with anyone after my break-up with Josh, my accident on the 134, the unraveling of it all, yet here I was laughing, completely at ease with this person. When Tilky turned to me and said, "You're my best friend," I believed him. I didn't see anyone else in his life showing up. And I sure didn't have anyone in my life making me feel like he did.

"Do NOT sleep with him," Sharise said, emphatically. "You can't let yourself get emotionally involved with Tilky, okay?"

I assured Sharise that sex was not on the table. As for emotional involvement, "Well, it's too late for that, Sharise," I said.

Tilky and I had already talked about what was happening between us, and like Sharise, he had concluded that sleeping together would be catastrophic. He was quite firm about that, whereas I, love junkie that I am, was offended that he didn't want to throw caution to the wind and embark on some ill-advised affair. I took it as a sign of my declining sexiness. I sobbed, looking at myself in the mirror and thinking, *I'm not pretty enough, am I?* Suddenly, I reminded myself of the pageant girls I used to laugh at back when I was a teenager. Back then, I wondered why they cared so damn much about how they looked, why their confidence was so fragile.

I totally get it now.

It took a few days for my ego to calm down. Then I realized that I had no real interest in disrupting our happy little friend zone. I wanted something better with him. I wanted to be buddies until the end of time. I wanted to play with his children one day, befriend his wife, be an ally and barbecue copilot. I just wanted to help him and make him feel better, and he could do the same for me.

This is meant to be, I told myself. *Clearly, he needed my help, that's why I was thinking about him so much that day. And I needed his help too. If he hadn't moved in here, I would have lost my home.*

Despite the safety and stability I'd given him and the healthy decision we'd made not to become lovers, Tilky was still making me feel a little nervous. He was charmingly liquored up most days, in a scruffy 1950s beat-poet-on-a-bender kind of way.

"It's okay. I can slow down. I can stop myself. It'll be okay," he reassured me. He was still heartbroken, he said, but soon it would get better. Being the daughter and ex-wife of drinkers, it was incredibly hard for me to believe he could actually just stop one day. I had to force myself not to panic, not to mother him. I had to stay focused on comedy. Because I had become very distracted since Tilky showed up in my home.

"You're not here on stage often enough," Jimmy told me. "If you really want to do comedy you have to get up each and every night."

I knew he was right. He had been doing comedy for thirteen years and he still did it three times a week, though he claimed even that was not enough.

But three times a week? I didn't know if I had that much funny in me.

"What would you say to someone who wants to be a baseball pro but never came to practice? You've got all the talent in the world, Bobbie, but where are you?"

***

SHARISE AND I WERE at my place, recording *The Sweet and Sour Hour*—a brand new podcast we were launching together. Tilky had made a little video of us, which I posted on my Instagram. You could clearly hear Tilky in the background speaking to us. Josh, who was now stalking me through a new fake Instagram account, saw the video and in a gesture of pure spite, tagged Leven in the comments, and sent me a bitchy DM.

"Oh, look what you're up to. You're such a good friend, huh? Oh yeah, now you're fucking her boyfriend?"

I wrote back to Josh, furious that he would drag poor Leven into his mind games.

"A) I'm not sleeping with anybody, and B) Mind your own fucking business."

As I sent Josh the "fuck off" message, Tilky lay on my bed next to me while Caroline sat on the couch, typing.

"I've known you for so fucking long, Bobbie," Tilky said.

"Uh-huh," I said, distracted. "How old were you when we met? Eighteen?"

"Twelve."

"Shut up."

"Hey, maybe I should also tell my entire life story to the world in a book."

"You should."

"But I'm scared. I'm private."

"Well, then don't talk about it."

"Let's do it. Let's start *right now*."

Caroline held up her voice recorder. "Ready when you are. So, what exactly happened with your ex? Was she cheating on you with the guy who played Tommy in the Mötley Crüe movie? 'Cause that would be so interesting and meta for the book."

Writers, I thought. *Very strange people.*

Tilky shook his head, sadly. "Nope. That's not what happened. It's a good movie, though. I was proud of her."

Tilky hadn't talked to Leven since the day they split up. He knew it was best not to, so they could both heal quicker.

"I have two other friends who are breaking up with girls and you know what they do?" he asked me. "Text them, call them. But I have to be stronger than that."

I wish I could be as disciplined as Tilky is, I thought, readying myself for a barrage of messages from Josh. My breakup with him felt like it was longer than the relationship, and I was starting to realize why. A part of me still craved the attention. I liked saying "no" to him because it was better than saying "no" to nobody. That's why I kept myself in this toxic loop. It was my ego. I was breadcrumbing him and he was love bombing me. We went back and forth, playing a pointless game of ping-pong neither of us would ever win.

THREE'S COMPANY

Before moving into my condo in Arleta, I had a place in Studio City that I shared with a girl named Sam[2]. While we were living together, she received some terrible news. Her mother had gone missing, and not long afterward, her body was found in Mexico. The murderer was never caught, and the death remains a mystery.

Sam's little sister, Chloe, took it especially hard.

"She's too much, I can't handle it," Sam said. She was on the phone with her sister, whom I could hear crying on the other end of line. Eventually, I went to the hotel where Chloe was staying and did my best to comfort her. Clearly, she needed a shoulder to cry on.

Around the same time Tilky moved into my condo, Chloe reached out and thanked me for being a such a good friend to her. She said she'd recently divorced and had moved to Los Angeles for a fresh start. She asked if I knew of any rooms available for rent as she was looking

---

Names have been changed.

for a place to live and had been couch-surfing with friends since arriving in LA.

And that's how a week after Tilky moved in, we found ourselves with a third roommate. Chloe, a thirty-six-year-old bartender and former tattoo shop owner whose heart was as broken as ours.

Sharise, as usual, had doubts about my decision. She had been trying to help me find roommates, setting up profiles for me on three different roommate-finding websites.

"This person is not going to be a good roommate for you, Bobbie," she said when I told her about Chloe moving in. "I can tell."

"But I want to help the girl. And Tilky doesn't mind."

"Bobbie, you need to live with someone who is a stranger and who has a stable job—preferably in the movie business because they work eighteen hours a day. Someone normal."

Sharise is really good at giving advice. And I'm really good at ignoring it.

Once Chloe moved in, every day felt like an episode of *Three's Company*—a trio of single people, each of us reeling from trauma and finding solace in one another. We also had a whole lotta fun. We'd go to Sally's Beauty Supply, cook food together, and at the end of the day we'd convene in my bedroom, the three of us giggling in bed wearing face masks, watching TV, or just talking. Chloe even had an eight-month-old male Chihuahua Piaf, who looked exactly like Nupa. As an added bonus, he and

Nupa were obsessed with one another. It was so sweet to watch.

Of course, having new people around always brings its challenges. Chloe, it turns out, had a habit of breaking appliances—specifically, my washing machine and dryer—and Tilky is no Mr. Fix-It. I didn't care, though. Broken appliances are a small price to pay for the sense of family Tilky and Chloe brought. My condo was no longer a lonely, dangerous place; it felt like a home. And best of all, I no longer had to go to comedy shows alone. Whether the show was good, not so good, or downright cringeworthy, they would be there cheering me on.

***

ONE NIGHT, MY EX Jay Gordon from the band Orgy, the Frankenscissors who once told me I wasn't funny, showed up at one of my shows. I was pleased he'd made the effort considering his lack of previous support for my comedy career. He showed up with a broken foot and said he was very excited to see me perform. My obsessive feelings for Jay had faded long ago, and I was glad we were friends. Also, what is it they say, success is the best revenge? That night I made sure I was extra confident on stage—a part of me wanted to show Jay just how wrong he'd been.

Back home, after the show, Tilky, Chloe, and I were in my bedroom, unwinding and listening to music. Chloe could not stop talking about Jay—turns out, she's a huge Orgy fan.

"Oh, my God! He's so cute, Bobbie, I love him!" she said.

"Yeah, he's pretty cool," I said.

"He's trying to hang out with you, Bobbie. I can tell. You should totally go for it. He's sooo hot."

"No, honey. Been there, done that."

"Yeah, but you guys used to have great sex, didn't you?"

I guess she must have read my book. Jay was the first man to make me orgasm from oral sex. No one before him—not Jani, not Tommy—had ever managed it. Jay and I had one of those strange, pheromonal connections. Even though he was a sulky cyber Goth who plucked his eyebrows and I was a blonde Valley mom who wore Uggs. In bed, we fit perfectly.

Speak of the devil—a message from Jay popped up on my phone.

"YOU WERE BRILLIANT TONIGHT. A GENIUS."

I showed it to Chloe, who smiled with a mischievous look in her eyes. Suddenly, she grabbed the phone out of my hands.

"What are you doing?" I asked.

"Nothing!" She hopped off the bed and ran into her bedroom.

Tilky and I looked at one another and shrugged. "She probably just wants to geek over Jay's messages," he said.

A few minutes later, Chloe came out of her room, a triumphant look on her face.

"Jay's on his way over."

"What are you talking about?" I said. "He'd better not be!"

"Yup, he's coming over."

"CHLOE! It's three a.m. and this is not happening!"

Before long, it was happening. Jay was outside the gate, ringing my door bell.

"Oh, my God, Tilky. He's here!"

"Open the door?" Tilky said.

"No! Let's pretend I'm asleep and can't hear."

Then the sound of footsteps coming up the stairs. Chloe had let him in.

"Shit! Lock the door!"

Tilky locked my bedroom door. Then, a soft knock.

"Bobbie? It's Jay. I'm here…"

I got into bed and pulled the covers over my head.

He kept knocking until Tilky, fed up, unlocked the door.

"Hi. Welcome."

Jay looked confused.

"Oh. Hi. Is Bobbie here?"

I peeked up from under the covers and pretended to be sleepy.

"Oh…Jay? What are you doing here?"

"Well. You told me to come over."

"I did?"

"She sure did," said Chloe, grinning.

"Yeah, and I said okay," said Jay.

"Oh, I didn't get that part. My phone must be dead."

"I was just working on Bobbie's computer, by the way," Tilky chimed in.

I looked at Tilky, then at Chloe, then at Jay.

"Well, I guess everyone's here now! I need a drink."

A few hours later, it was past 5:00 a.m., and everyone was still in my room. Chloe was making goo-goo eyes at Jay while Tilky was looking up YouTube videos on my computer.

Jay whispered to me, "Are they ever going to leave?"

By this point, I just wanted to get in bed too, whether Jay was with me or not.

"Guys, it's getting late," I announced.

Chloe and Tilky looked at one another, then got up and left the room. As soon as the door closed behind them, Jay pulled me up off the floor and threw me on the bed, kissing me passionately.

"Bobbie, you're so beautiful. And you're funny, it's so fucking hot!"

Oh, my gosh. *Was Jay my first chucklefucker?*

Tilky walked in the room, a deadpan look on his face. Without saying a word, he walked up to Jay and I, and held his phone in Jay's face—a photo of a cantaloupe being fingered, the insides oozing out. Then he turned around and walked out.

"What the hell was that about?" I yelled after him.

"Who cares?" said Jay, getting back to eating my face, slowly working his way down until his head was between my legs. His mouth was performing its signature move, the dance of the silver tongue. Back in the 2000s, I was powerless against that tongue. But this was 2018, at five thirty in the morning, and the tongue had lost its luster. There was no way I was going to orgasm. I just wanted this long night to be over.

"We're going to have sex, Bobbie," said Jay, coming up for air.

I had to think fast. "Don't you have to drop your daughter at school in an hour?" I said. "I mean, I'd hate to rush things, you know? After all this time."

He looked at me, fire in his eyes.

"You're right. We can't rush this moment. Call me later, I'll come back. We'll pick up right where we left off." He put on his clothes, kissed me passionately, and left.

Within minutes I was asleep, Nupa curled on the pillow next to me.

The next day, after Jay's unexpected visit, I asked Tilky what was up with the cantaloupe video. He shrugged and admitted the whole thing had felt a little strange for him. He was used to being the only man in the house. I gave him a hug and told him not to worry. I had no intention of inviting Jay back into my bedroom. I'd had a taste of chucklefucking, and frankly, it was exhausting.

MARSH GASSES

IT WAS THE WEEK before Christmas and I was back in Baton Rouge about to perform my homecoming show at the Comedy Étouffée club.

It was a nightmare right off the bat. Taylar's fiancé drove us there and had to keep circling the venue, round and round, looking for parking. Patience is not my best virtue, and I actually screamed at him to stop so I could get out and just get into the club. When I did, my heart sank—there was no green room where I could prepare, no VIP room nor designated area for me to sign books, merch, or give autographs. Just a huge sea of faces from my childhood, judging me. At least that's how it felt.

I pulled my mother aside in a panic. "I can't talk nasty in front of these people! They all know me: it's going to be so embarrassing!"

My mom, for her part, did her very best to calm me down. "Bobbie, this is what you do. Look at these people as dollar bills. You need to make them laugh because that's what they paid for. Please don't worry about embarrassing yourself or your family. In fact, I'd encourage it."

"I'm freaking out, Mom. I can't even remember any of my jokes!"

"Do the one about having sex that sounds like you're running in flip-flops, I love that one. The one about the guy's testicle coming out of his pants, I'm not crazy about that one. You should do the one about doing head on that guy where he's having a seizure—I like that."

The stage was only about a foot higher than the floor. Once I stepped on it, there was no escaping the sea of faces from my past. The little boys who chased me on the playground were now grown men. My best friend from dance class. The girls from high school. Old boyfriends. Neighbors. I'm pretty sure all the Tiger Droppings guys were there—theparadigm, kingbob, BuckyCheese, Hot-Carl—hoping to catch a whiff of White Diamonds. And in the front row, my entire Goddamn family minus the Minnesota contingent—my mother, my stepfather William Williamson, Taylar, and her fiancé. I was so grateful to see them.

I nervously lifted the mic to my lips, and got to joking.

I was in a really good place earlier. Well, actually it was a liquor store. And nothing says "I mean business" like using a shopping cart at a liquor store. I ran out of coffee that morning, and I thought tequila seemed like a reasonable replacement. People can call me an addict, but I say it's not "addiction" until you've sucked a dick for it. Right?

Find the funny, Bobbie, find the funny…

The other night, my boyfriend said, 'Sorry for calling you a whore all those times. I didn't realize a lack of love from your parents leaves a hole in your heart only dicks can fill.'

The people in the room looked shocked. There was nothing intelligent coming out of my mouth except a jumbled mess of one-liners that I'm sure had sounded good at some point, but not in this order. Only now did I finally concede that Jimmy, Sharise, and Jamie had been right about doing a new set for each show. It was bullshit. A mistake. I only wished I could have figured it out sooner. If I hadn't been so full of piss and vinegar, so prideful, maybe I wouldn't be on stage right now humiliating myself in front of my entire hometown.

I will say this, though. My favorite part of the body has got to be the taint. I call it "the silky skin highway from hole to hole."

I looked around the room and saw a lot of open mouths. I am blunt; I am crude; I think farts are funny; I am a thirteen-year-old boy trapped in a woman's body. And I'm not sure that's what they expected. They wanted the Cherry Pie Girl. But didn't they know that wasn't me?

A lone heckler yelled, "Show us your tits!"

Fuck you, kingbob. It was time to roll out the big guns.

So the other day I go out and have sex with the first man I see. We get naked and immediately I'm like, oh shit, he's FULLY HAIRY! This guy is so hairy, when he goes to wipe, it's like peanut butter stuck in a shag carpet! I'm not going to suggest he needed a pube trimmer, but when you get an erection and it looks like Pinocchio joined the Taliban, you gotta ask yourself, is it time?

My mother might have laughed, but no one else did. *This is awful, and I want to die.* This crowd was more intimidating than any other. More so than the people in Hollywood. The actors and the jokers, the entertainment industry people and the people buying VIP tickets—I didn't care about them. I didn't care if some agent thought I was hot stuff, or some producer thought he could "package" me into some showbiz product. But I cared about this. About showing my mom and Taylar and all the folks I grew up with that I was funny, that I was cool, that I hadn't made a mistake when I left Baton Rouge and moved to Hollywood and let down every person that loved me because of my own fear and weakness. *This* was the audience I cared about most. And I was terrified that I was about to let them down again.

My friend is such a slut that when she eats a hotdog she puts a hand behind her head. When she burps I smell cock and bacon. Her favorite color is dick, and when she has sex, it's like throwing a hotdog down a hallway.

Then, I felt it coming for me. That strange floating feeling, the one I'd managed to avoid since my first two shows. As a series of random thoughts spilled un-controllably from my lips, I tried to use all the techniques Jimmy had taught me to stay present. But as I launched into a joke about how the light at the end of the tunnel is just us being pushed out of another vagina, I began to drift away, and I stopped trying to fight it. I welcomed it.

I left my body and traveled deep into the Southern night, the air laden with the scent of creole seasoning, blackened shrimp, my dad's old aftershave and Winstons, the sounds of blues guitar and Pink Anderson singing *I got a woman, way across town*...I floated, glided into the swamp, toward the faint glow of gasses burning in the marsh...

I heard the soft voice of my father: *Bobbie...I'm gonna show you how to play the blues...*

***

DESPITE THE HORRIBLE SHOW I put on for my good Southern brethren, Christmas in Baton Rouge with my mom and my daughter had been shaping up to be one of the best I'd ever had. Not just because of the warm sense of belonging that always envelops me the second I step foot on my mom's porch, but because for the first time in years, leaving that porch behind wouldn't feel like a mistake.

Yes, they teased me about my performance—most of which I could not remember—but they also insisted they'd enjoyed it, even if no one else in the audience did. Taylar was so supportive it made me cry.

"I could never get up in front of a big crowd and do stand-up," she said. "But you're brave enough to do it, and you're actually good at it. I'm so proud. I'll still be proud whether this turns into a real career for you or not. I really hope it does."

It meant so much that she believed in me. That my whole family had been there, cheering on my ridiculousness. For the first time in years, my mom and daughter were able to enjoy my life choices. Finally, why I had to be in LA made sense to them. LA was no longer just a place where Bobbie went to take care of some man. LA was now a place where Bobbie was finally growing into her best self.

✳✳✳

TILKY HAD STAYED IN LA while I was gone and then spent Christmas with some friends on the East Coast. Every time I started to worry about him, I checked myself. I wasn't his girlfriend, and I wasn't his mom—I was his friend. All I could do was believe in him. Nothing more, nothing less.

When he called and said he missed me, my mom chimed in. "Tell him he's welcome to come here."

So on his way back to LA, Tilky stopped by Baton Rouge.

The night he arrived we all went to dinner.

"He used to be in a boy band," I explained to my mom before we sat down.

"Doesn't mean jack to me," she said, on point as always. "All I want to know is, is he a good person, Bobbie? Does he pull his weight? You've been waiting on him hand and foot."

"I've been treating him as I would any other guest in our home!"

Mom was, naturally, protective of me, and that's why she'd invited Tilky to Baton Rouge. She'd seen too often what can happen when I let someone new into my life. Someone who's younger, needs help and love.

"You know how you are, Bobbie. Sometimes people use you, sometimes they are cruel."

"He's not my boyfriend, Mom! We're just friends!"

"Yes, and sometimes you fall in love with them anyway, without even noticing that's what you're doing. You've got a huge heart and it's easy to get in there."

We went to dinner in town, and my half-sister, Amy, went absolutely gaga over Tilky, as all women do.

"Well, God, son," my mom said. "Bobbie's gonna get jealous that you're giving all your attention to her sister."

My mouth gaped. "Mom, shut *up*!"

My mom looked at my stepdad. "It's so obvious Bobbie's into him, isn't it? He's a real pussy charmer!"

"Mom, with all respect, BE QUIET."

"Oh, I'm just pickin' at him," she said.

"You're not pickin' at him, you're pickin' at *me*!"

When I looked at Tilky, he was laughing. Harder than he had in months.

"What is it?" I asked him.

"I'm the pussy charmer!"

My mom turned to me and winked. "This one's all right, Bobbie. I like him."

THIS IS A MAM'S WORLD

Finally, I had stability at home. Great friends around me. Josh was totally out of my life. And I had found my raison d'être in comedy. It's amazing how quickly things can shift. Three months ago, I was bottoming out, questioning my existence, rudderless. Now life felt hopeful. Exciting, even. I had a path. The only piece missing from the puzzle was a man.

My phone pinged with a message from a guy I had a date with that night. He was older (meaning my age) and an entertainment attorney (meaning not broke), so I had high hopes. It couldn't be any worse than the last couple of dates I'd been on. There was the guy from Bumble who worked at Disney and couldn't stop talking about his ex.

"My ex, we just had an instant connection."

I nodded, chewing on a rib. "Uh huh."

"We really loved each other right off the bat. It happened so fast."

"Cool."

"Then, out of nowhere, she broke up with me. Can you believe that, Bobbie? She thought things were moving too fast, but *she* was the one who said 'I love you' first."

I wished I could shove a rib into his mouth to shut him up.

The next Bumble disaster was a full two inches shorter than me. He *also* spent most of the evening talking about the ex-girlfriend who broke his heart. "She was so beautiful, just like you," he said. "Do you want to see her picture?"

"That's okay," I said, mouth full of sushi.

"Bobbie, oh, my God, you have such great skin! Let's take a selfie." We took a selfie. Then he continued to grill me for advice on how to win back his ex.

"Just stop being a pushover, bro," I said, waving for the check.

The next day, he texted me.

"Thank you sooo much for being my friend! I'm going to take all the advice you gave me! And I'm going to Photoshop our photos so you look PERFECT!!! Drink soon?"

I blame Sharise for getting me back on the dating apps. In her opinion, modern love is a numbers game. She says if you go out with ten guys, you're bound to like one of them. But I found the whole rigmarole exhausting. I really, really hoped tonight's date with the entertainment attorney would suck less than the last two. I read his message:

"Hey, instead of dinner, let's see this live show my friend is putting on…starts at 9."

A show? On a first date? I was hoping for something more intimate.

"I'm not really up for a late night tonight. I'm flying to Minnesota early tomorrow. Do you mind if we just stick to dinner?"

"Let's just reschedule then. I don't like early nights…"

And I don't like assholes. I didn't even bother replying.

I showed Tilky the messages and he shook his head, disappointed. "What a tool! Why don't you come to the party with me and Juliette tonight instead?"

Juliette was the twenty-year-old actress he'd been seeing for a few weeks. I'd already pranked her a few times and she'd taken it well, so I knew she was cool. The first night she stayed over, I planted a remote-control turd in Tilky's bedroom while they were downstairs cooking, and in the middle of the night, I started driving the turd around his room. In the morning, when she was in the shower, I took my airhorn, stuck it around the bathroom door, and blasted it. From then on she was officially part of the family. I liked her for Tilky; he seemed happy, and that made me happy too.

We went to her roommate's birthday party that night, which was much more fun than feeling sorry for myself at home. I gave the birthday girl a little present and chatted with Tilky.

"I think I'm ready to meet my guy now," I told him.

"He's not here, is he?" Tilky said, looking around.

"No. But I'm glad I came." I left the party early, in much better spirits than before.

On my way back to Arleta, I noticed I was low on gas, so I pulled into a gas station and started filling up. A man standing by his Range Rover was looking at me. He was tall and well built, like a slimline version of The Rock, and I wasn't mad when he walked over and started chatting me up.

"Pardon me, but I don't think I've seen anything so beautiful in all my life," he said with a British accent.

I looked behind me and said coyly, "Do you mean me?"

"Have we met before? Were you on television?"

"Yes, a few years ago. I was on a show called *Ex Wives of Rock*."

He smiled. "Oh. I know Lorraine." Lorraine Lewis was my friend, and the show's producer. Small world...

"Are you single?"

"Yes."

"Would you like not to be?"

"I don't know..."

"Can I have your number?"

"Can I ask what your name is?"

"It's Mams. Mams Taylor."

Mams Taylor...what a name. What a dream boat.... The universe must have been listening! That's why my stupid date with the jerky entertainment attorney had fallen through. If I hadn't been here at this gas station, I would never have met him...*Mams*.

I went home and immediately Googled Mams. According to TMZ.com, Mams is a little bit of a bad boy, which as we all know is my preferred genre. He knocked out Jesse Metcalfe with one punch. He wrote a song for Carmen Electra called "Bigger Dick." He's also associated with the musical genre "runk." I had never heard of "runk," but it sounded like a mix of punk and drunk, which was fine by me.

I called Sharise and told her the good news about Mams. Her reaction, though, was surprising. As soon as I told her his name, she started screaming.

"NOO!!!! NOOO!!!!"

"Sharise, what is it? What's wrong?

"NOOOOO!"

"TELL ME!"

"NOOOOOOO!"

"He's rich, he's famous, he dates hot chicks. How does that make him a 'no'?"

"Bobbie, he was on the first season of *Ex Wives*, don't you remember?"

"He was?"

"He's my baby daddy's piece-of-shit best friend. He's a nightmare. A total player. YOU CANNOT DATE HIM."

"Oh."

I promised Sharise I wouldn't go out with Mams, but when he slid into my DMs later that night, I have to admit, I felt a little tingle of excitement in my belly.

"I want to see you."

He was direct. To the point. I liked that. No endless texting back and forth. No mixed signals, no breadcrumbs here. I typed back:

"Me too."

He seemed like a smooth kind of guy. I imagined him picking me up in his Range Rover, taking me to a beautiful restaurant. In Malibu. Maybe my hair would blow in the wind on the PCH as we drove up there. I better start planning my outfit.

"When?"

I bit my lip with anticipation as the little bubbles showed him typing his response. There would be champagne. Lingering eye contact as we clinked our glasses, looks that hinted at romance. Then his answer arrived.

"Now."

Now? Was this a booty call? The veil lifted on my short-lived fantasy of finding true love with a dashing Brit. I realized that I wasn't messaging with Mams. I was actually messaging with his boner. And when conversing with boners, I've found it's best to be very clear and direct.

"I don't do 'now.'"

And that was the last I heard from Mams.

Sharise was right about him. Go figure.

BOBBIE BROWN'S KILLER SET

THERE AREN'T MANY FIRSTS left for me, but until I flew to Minnesota to visit my brother in his new home, I'd never been in the snow before. I'd *seen* snow. But I'd never been *in* it. I'd never made a snowman, or thrown a snowball, or touched it with my bare hands. Neither had my nephew, Ollie, and together, we made a snowman, threw real snowballs, and made an igloo and snow angels too. Laughing while lying on my back and waving my arms and legs up and down to make the first snow angel of my life, I couldn't help but feel that my brother had made the right decision. They were much better off out here than in LA.

We sat at the dinner table with his parents, and Ollie whispered to me, "You're my favorite aunt," and I just wanted to eat him up. Then he glanced over at his mom and dad, who were flirting with one another across the table, still very much in love.

"Um, hey, you guys are starting to get gross," he said, and we all laughed.

"He's got your sense of humor, Bobbie," Adam said.

I was sad to leave Minnesota, especially because there was a little tension at home in Arleta. Just a few little red flags here and there with Chloe. Sometimes we'd rub each other the wrong way. And I was having a little bit of an issue with her dog, Piaf. Don't get me wrong, I love dogs. Believe it or not, before *Dirty Rocker Boys* came out, I worked as a personal assistant at a talent agency for dogs, and it was one of the most fun jobs I've ever had. But Piaf, handsome and charming a young man as he was, had some issues.

He wasn't really house-trained even though Chloe had sworn he was, and for some reason he had decided that my room was the toilet. Each time he marked my carpet with a number one or two, Nupa would do the polite thing and match it with a gift of her own. It was getting gross, and I was sick of shampooing the carpet three times a day. Piaf and Nupa also seemed to be developing feelings for one another. Despite the pronounced age difference—he was one, she was ten—he was acting like she was his bitch, and frankly, she seemed into it. He'd started humping her. Because he wasn't fixed and neither was Nupa, it was really becoming an issue. The relationship unfolding in my bedroom was a strange, smelly, dangerous affair, and it had to stop.

Things hit a low point when Jay invited me to an Orgy show and I made the mistake of mentioning it to ultra-fan Chloe. Jay never confirmed the passes, and I'd developed a raging migraine in the meantime, so I just decided not to go. But Chloe, who'd gotten it in her head that she was going to rage backstage with her heroes, was furious and yelled at me for letting her down. The next day, when Piaf shat in my room again, I decided it was time to have a proper talk. Redraw some boundaries. Clear the shit-scented air.

I knocked on Chloe's door, and the second she opened it, it became clear she had no interest in having an adult conversation.

"You're MEAN," she said. "You've been MEAN to me since the SECOND I moved in! You treat me like a tenant, not a friend."

"Well, you are my tenant. And I was hoping we could *become* friends…"

"YOU'RE FUCKING EVIL, BOBBIE! YOU'VE NEVER BEEN NICE TO ME!"

Her ferocity took me by surprise.

"Chloe, this has got to be the most ungrateful thing I have ever heard. And you know, ingratitude is what holds people back in life."

She folded her arms, glowering. "You promised me we were going to the Orgy show."

"I never promised you anything."

"And you're mean to Piaf."

"I love Piaf, but you weren't very honest when you said he was totally house-trained. Every time he comes in my room, he shits or pees or both, and then Nupa has to remark his markings. It's gross."

"*You're* gross. Look at you. Fifty years old and renting out rooms to people half your age. I feel sorry for you."

And there they were: her true colors. The ones Sharise had seen from day one. I made a mental note to stop ignoring Sharise's advice. And I wasn't going to let myself lose my temper. Not today, Satan. Not today.

"Whatever, I've found a new apartment anyway," she spat.

"Well, thanks for the notice, and good for you! You broke my washing machine and dryer by the way. Are you going to pay to get those fixed?"

"Get the fuck out of my face, Bobbie."

Then she put her hands on me, shoved me into the hallway, and slammed the door shut in my face.

For a few seconds I couldn't move. Then, a strange sound, a yelping, began emanating from my room. I ran in to the horrifying sight of Piaf having full, consensual sex with my Nupa.

"NO!" I screamed, trying to separate them. "BAD DOGS!"

But their bodies were locked together in some diabolical tango. Nupa looked at me with the "sorry not sorry" face that she usually reserved for after she'd shat on my rugs.

I called Taylar, thinking that her job at the dog boarding and grooming facility would mean she could give me some advice. "What do I do? How do I get them apart? Is there a morning after pill for dogs?"

"Mom, listen to me," said Taylar. "When dogs mate, the male's penis swells up inside the female's vagina, so it's totally normal for them to get stuck together. Do NOT try to divide them, you could hurt them both."

I watched Nupa standing there, attached butt to butt with Piaf like it was no big deal. I had to give it to Mother Nature, she sure has a weird sense of humor.

"How long are they locked together like this?

"Like fifteen, twenty minutes. He's ejaculating inside her right now, see?"

"EW! Taylar, what if she gets pregnant? She's too old for this shit!"

A beep indicated I had a call waiting—it was Caroline.

"Shit, Taylar, I have to get this." I switched the calls over. "Caroline, you are not going to believe what's happening…" I told her about Chloe, and could hear Caroline's little fingers typing while she took notes on the other end.

"Bobbie, this is wonderful. You really are the gift that keeps on giving!"

"I thought I had stability in my home life, Caroline. And now it's just the same old bullshit. I can't stand this drama. It just follows me wherever I go!"

"Bobbie, listen to me, if anything else completely dramatic and hilarious happens to you in the next twenty-four hours, you tell me straight away, okay? Really, this is all great!"

"Great? It doesn't feel that way."

"Depends how you look at it, Bobbie. From a comedic perspective, it's gold."

I hung up the phone and looked at Nupa, who looked happier than I'd ever seen her, walking around with her boy toy attached to her like a backpack. *Like mother like daughter. Ugh.*

***

A FEW WEEKS LATER, I was at home working on my set when I heard Tilky come in the door from his film shoot. He'd been gone a couple of days, and so far I'd spared him news of the drama that had been unfolding with our roommate.

Tilky came upstairs and knocked on my door.

"Sit down, I have some news," I told him.

He sat on the edge of the bed, next to me.

"Chloe's moving out. It got ugly."

"What?"

"And there's something else."

Nupa was lying in my lap. She'd been pining for Piaf all day. I picked her up and handed her to Tilky. He cradled her gently.

"What is it, Bobbie?"

"We went to the vet.

"Oh, my God, she's not sick is she?"

"No. She's pregnant, Tilky. We're having a baby."

Earlier that day, Nupa's vet had confirmed that following her night of passion with Piaf, Nupa was with child. I had assumed that because of Nupa's advanced age— she's around eighty-five in dog years—she'd be unable to carry a pregnancy to term. But the vet told me otherwise. Apparently Nupa was perfectly capable of bearing a litter, so long as I had the commitment and responsibility required to become a grandmother. I looked at Nupa, who had been crying for Piaf nonstop. As a woman, a mother, and a certified codependent, I knew exactly what she was going through. She loved her hot young man. And she wanted his puppies.

Nupa snuggled down on Tilky's lap as he took it all in. He promised me that no matter what, he'd be there for us, like we'd been there for him when he needed it. Soon, it would no longer be just the three of us. It would be the five, maybe the six of us. Nupa, sensing the love that surrounded her, started to fall asleep. She seemed a little more tired than usual, but otherwise, glowing.

***

I WAS SCRIBBLING AWAY at the desk in my room in Arleta.

According to a comedic theory developed by author William Lang, there are only three parts to most comedic bits. S = Setup, A = Anticipation, and P = Punch line. SAP. Every story needs a payoff. A satisfying conclusion. Hm.

I met a guy who said his last girlfriend was the craziest bitch he'd ever met. I said, "Challenge accepted."

I looked at the pages for a second, tore them out of my notebook, and placed them in a folder called "BOBBIE BROWN'S KILLER SET."

I hadn't talked to Jimmy in a week or so, since he'd put me on the Comedy Store schedule really, really late. I was on after midnight, after the headliner, the dead hour when rookies and the waitresses and staff get up on stage and most of the audience has already gone home. Having always headlined or coheadlined up 'til then, playing to a tired, empty room was a shock to my diva sensibilities. There was no crowd to speak of, except for my poor friends who had been there for six hours waiting, wondering when the hell I was going on. By the time I did, everyone was either drunk, half-asleep, or over it.

Afterward, I cornered Jimmy, in full Bobbie the Bulldog attack mode. "FUCK TO THE NO, JIMMY!" I yelled, "Don't *ever* do that to me again!"

He smiled patiently, as usual. "This is what it's about, Bobbie. You've gotta get up, every night. Whether you're in front of a hundred people, or five. You've gotta get up. That's how you get good."

✳✳✳

Tilky popped his head around my bedroom door. He looked good; it was his first day shooting a movie, and he'd been working hard all weekend, studying the script.

"Hey, thanks for the worm by the way," he said.

I had planted a fake plastic earthworm in his charcoal face wipes because, well, the day didn't feel complete unless I'd pranked Tilky.

"What are you doing today?" he asked.

"Just working on these jokes; I've really hit a wall. The last few shows have sucked, big time. I need new jokes, better jokes…"

"Bobbie, can I be real with you?" Tilky asked. "Sometimes you're funnier in real life than when you do stand-up."

"I am?"

"Yeah. Next time you're on stage, just pretend you're telling me a story. Trust me."

I thought about it for a while. Surely it couldn't be that simple?

My phone pinged—it was a text message from Jamie Kennedy. We hadn't spoken since the incident at the Dojo. I waved goodbye to Tilky, wished him good luck on set, and opened the text.

"I'm ready for your apology," it said.

I sneaked a quick peek at his Instagram—he was wearing the sweaters I got him. *The nerve!* I screen-grabbed a few of the photos and sent them to him with my response.

"Stepping up your fashion game, I see…"

Jamie apologized for being out of touch. He said his mother had been ill and that it had been a difficult time. Whatever wounded feelings I had immediately evaporated. Family's more important than any of this shit.

"I'm so sorry, Jamie. I'm here for you."

I wasn't sure if he'd respond; his track record suggested it would take him eight to twelve hours to get back to me. But he wrote back straight away.

"Thank you."

Then Jimmy called—he had a cancellation that night at the Dojo, would I be up for performing?

"Yeah. Let's do it. Sign me up."

This was the day. I was going to try something new. I was going to tell 'em stories, like Tilky said. Open up. Be myself. What else is there? I'd been playing a role, the

Cherry Pie Girl, my whole life. Now, with comedy, I had a chance to move beyond that. And I was going to take it. Tonight.

✳✳✳

THAT NIGHT, I GOT up on the stage with Tilky, Juliette, Gretchen, and Sharise in the front row. All of them looking at me with "you got this" expressions on their faces. I took a deep breath and started talking.

"It's no secret in Hollywood that I've been trying to quit my addiction to sex with younger men. My dog, on the other hand…"

I relaxed and took my time telling the story. Fleshed it out into a good ol' yarn, as if I was chatting to my best friend. Or my dad. Just a little kitchen banter among family. I took it easy, invited the audience to get involved, and by the time I got to the part of the story where Nupa's pregnancy test came back positive, the whole room was rolling with laughter. Dare I say it, I think I was better than the headliner. Jimmy came up to me backstage, delighted.

"Bobbie, that was a breakthrough performance! Really killer. Your best set ever."

Seemed like I was getting closer and closer to cracking the code. I knew it was going to take time, I knew I still had work to do. But that night, I had turned a corner. Who needs sex, drugs, and rock 'n' roll, anyway?

I was high on that feeling for days.

CODA
THE LAST WORD

So, as you know, I love to have the last word. That much hasn't changed, and maybe it never will. That fact is among a few other things I'm trying to accept about myself. Like the fact that I'm still single. That I'm still shy about meeting new men. That I'm still scared of being lied to and getting hurt. That after a lifetime of lessons, there's still so much to learn.

Every day, I try to be grateful for all of my good fortune, and for my loved ones. And when I wonder why life still feels unsettled, I remind myself that some creatures are meant to live in motion. Some of us are meant to hustle hard every day. We're meant to pursue our dreams, not just to make ends meet, but because that's what keeps us alive and vibrant. The longest relationship I've had has been with my dreams. Perhaps they've been my soulmate all along.

So I'll plow ahead with this new idea, dive into that new career option, and on or off stage, search for the funny. Because there's a punchline to nearly every story, if you're brave enough to wait for it.

Be patient, work, strive, and hold on, no matter how bleak things may seem, because the dark times can take us to the brightest places. The people who hurt us can teach us valuable lessons. Our struggles are what give us the strength and wisdom necessary for individual growth. Our losses make room in our hearts for the most wonderful new people to enter. Curses can be blessings in disguise, and dead ends can push you onto a completely new path. There's always hope to be found if we seek it. As long as there are people who love you, you will always be okay. If there's no one around to love you, well, love yourself.

You're sure to come out on top.

Love, Bobbie xo

Acknowledgments

THANK YOU TO GRETCHEN Bonaduce for helping me make this second book a reality. To Caroline for "getting me" and being my partner in this book writing journey. To Taylar for understanding her crazy mom and always helping her "grow up." To my mom, Judy, and stepdad, Mr. Billy, for their unyielding support and advice. To everyone at Rare Bird for believing in my story and continuing to give it life. To my new friends in comedy who help me find the funny. To my brother, Adam, his wife, Laura, and my nephew and little lobster, Ollie, for reminding me what it means to be in an amazing family and the meaning of joy again after so long. Thank you, all. I love you.